THE COMPLETE E   F

Decorative
Paint Effects

30 creative ideas to transform your home

NEW
HOLLAND

First published in 1996 by
New Holland Publishers (UK) Ltd
London • Cape Town • Sydney • Auckland
www.newhollandpublishers.com

Garfield House, 86-88 Edgware Road
London W2 2EA
United Kingdom

80 McKenzie Street
Cape Town 8001
South Africa

Level 1, Unit 4
Suite 411, 14 Aquatic Drive
Frenchs Forest, NSW 2086
Australia

Unit 1A, 218 Lake Road
Northcote, Auckland
New Zealand

10 9 8 7 6 5

ISBN 1 84330 214 4

Editor: Emma Callery
Designer: Jerry Goldie
Photographers: Sue Atkinson,
Tony Buckley, Zul Mukhida,
Heini Scheebeli, Jon Stewart,
Steve Tanner, Shona Wood

Reproduction by Pica Digital Pte Ltd, Singapore
Printed and bound by Times Offset (M) Sdn Bhd

A note of warning

Many of the projects in this book include the use of ceramic paints. Purpose-made cold ceramic paints for the home hobbyist are non-toxic and therefore safe for general use. However, they do not conform to food safety regulations, and should on no account be used on objects that will come into contact with your mouth, nor should food be served from surfaces decorated with such paints. Ceramic paints are meant for decorative rather than utilitarian purposes and objects painted with them will not withstand repeated use unless treated with respect.

Water-based paints resist scratches and are much harder wearing than solvent-based ones. Objects decorated with ceramic paints should be gently hand-washed in warm water using a mild detergent. Under no circumstances should you wash them in a dish washer, nor are you advised to soak them for too long in soapy water.

You can buy clear glaze to protect solvent-based ceramic paints - allow the paint to dry thoroughly before applying a coat. Inevitably, however, the extra protective coat will be visible and may detract from the appeal of fine paint work. If you are decorating objects which will not be used to eat and drink from, then you need not worry about whether or not the paint is toxic. For this reason, you can use spray paint or enamel paints, which are much harder wearing. The irony, of course, is that such objects will need cleaning far less often, so ceramic paints could equally be used.

Contents

Introduction

Through using decorative paint effects, bringing colour into your home is made so simple, so immediate, so vital, that once you have created some of the projects in this book you will want to keep on doing so. All you need do is arm yourself with an assortment of paintbrushes and paint pots, read through the step-by-step text and – hey presto! – you will have a sponged tea service, a stencilled picture mount, or an oak-patterned chair. These are just three of the projects in this book, and there are a further twenty-seven waiting to be discovered.

Paint is such a flexible medium that you can use it on almost any surface. Wood, ceramics, and paper spring most readily to mind, but how about fabric, or painting over silver leaf to give the impression of water gilding in gold leaf? This last effect may sound quite exotic, but the paint effect that is used to achieve it is really most straightforward – just like each of the techniques featured here. These include sponging, stippling, colourwashing and stencilling, and are readily achieved on different items around the house.

To make this book as easy as possible to use, there is an introductory chapter on materials, equipments and basic techniques and then the projects are divided into rooms to give you ideas for their setting. So, Living Rooms includes a stencilled chintz cushion and a wondrously colourful papier mâché bowl; among other ideas, Kitchens and Bathrooms show how to stencil tiles and make an abstract roller blind; in Bedrooms you will find how to paint a country armoire or block print bedlinen, and in Nurseries there are instructions for a beautifully simple cat toy box and a chicken cushion.

Discover how a simple stencil pattern was used for the Lemon-painted Table on page 66

Each of the projects has numerous step-by-step photographs to accompany the text which shows exactly how to make or paint each element. In addition, there is also a photograph of the finished piece in situ to inspire and inform you. What more could you ask for? Now is the time to begin painting all those items you have always intended to brighten up - there really is nothing like a lick of paint, especially one with a decorative effect.

Materials and Equipment

The projects in this book employ a variety of techniques to achieve the finished effect. While the text and photographs illustrate the stages involved in each design, you might nevertheless find it useful to refer to this section. It comprises a comprehensive and alphabetical list of the materials and equipment used in the projects that follow later in the book.

Agate burnisher

This is a small piece of agate stone mounted in a handle; it is rubbed over water gilded leaf to give a high shine.

Carbon paper

Thin sheets of paper, one side of which is coated in carbon. Commonly used to provide a reference copy when typing letters, in some of the projects in this book it is used to transfer pre-drawn designs onto ceramic objects and furniture by placing the paper, carbon-side down, onto the ceramic surface and tracing around the design (see Basic Techniques, page 12). Carbon paper is usually dark (black, royal blue or purple), and this is what you will need when transferring designs onto white glazed ceramics. However, you can also buy white carbon paper, which you may find you need if you are transferring onto ceramics with a dark glaze.

Gesso

Gesso, or whiting, is a chalk powder used as the base for producing gesso solution, the first coat of gesso and putty. Ready-mixed acrylic gesso is also available.

Gilder's pad, knife and tip

These are used together to lay loose leaf. The leaf is laid on a soft pad (surrounded by a parchment or paper screen to shield against draughts), and, if necessary, is cut using the knife. A round-ended kitchen knife can be used if it is free from nicks in the blade. The tip – a soft, wide brush – is used to pick up the leaf and lay it on the surface to be decorated.

Agate burnisher

Gilder's tips

Gilder's knife

1-1/2" ROBERSON'S GILDERS TIP

4" ROBERSON'S GILDERS TIP DOUBLE THICKNESS

Petroleum jelly may be used to add extra adherence to the tip (see step 3, page 46) making it easier to use.

Gilding water
This liquid is used to attach loose leaf gold or silver in water gilding. It is mixed from cold water, methylated spirit (wood alcohol) and heated rabbit-skin size (see also step 3, page 46).

Marker pen
A pen with a fine nib, usually used in this book to mark off points around the rim of a ceramic object. Graphic designers' pens (available from art and specialist stores) are best, since the nibs are very fine. Black ink is most suitable for marking, but try to find a pen in which the ink is not waterproof. If you have difficulty removing the marks with water, try using a small amount of neat turpentine on a clean piece of tissue.

Masking fluid
Usually sold as Water Colour Art Masking Fluid, this is used to mask out areas on ceramics to be protected when painting, and contains rubber latex and ammonia. Make sure the surface is clean and dry, shake the masking fluid bottle well, and apply to the surface with a paintbrush (see Basic Techniques, page 13). Masking fluid is toxic and should be stored away safely. Always clean the paintbrush and wash your hands thoroughly immediately after use.

Masking paper
A transparent 'film' of self-adhesive paper, with a waxed paper backing that peels away. It is commonly available in art shops, and is also sold by stationery and office suppliers. The paper is often sold as a protective covering to be applied to book covers, maps and other documents. For some of the projects in this book, it is used to mask out areas you wish to remain blank while painting.

Masking tape
A self-adhesive tape, usually pale yellow, used in home decorating to protect edges around door frames, light switches and so on when painting. It is particularly useful if you want to paint a hard, crisp edge.

Metal straight edge
Use to mark out straight lines on cardboard pieces, and as a cutting edge for clean straight finishes.

Paints
There are two basic types of paint, water-based (emulsion, vinyl enamel or latex), and oil-based. Both varieties come in a flat/matt, satin or gloss finish. For painting furniture, a flat or matt finish paint is most preferable, as decorative work will adhere better to a duller basecoat. A gloss shine can always be applied after the decoration using a poly-gloss varnish.

Although oil-based paints tend to render a more brilliant colour with a stronger finish, water-based paints are easier to work with, as they can be thinned with water, and require only warm, soapy water for clearing up and washing brushes. Oil-based paints require a solvent, such as white (mineral) spirit, for thinning and cleaning (see page 9). Whereas an oil-based paint will take anywhere from 8 to 12 hours to dry, a water-based coat will generally dry in less than 2 to 3 hours.

With all paints, allow each coat to dry thoroughly before applying successive coats, as the damp layer may wrinkle or bubble under the new layer if it is not allowed full drying time. With

Gilder's pad and gold leaf

Tracing paper

Gesso

Masking fluid

Carbon paper

Metal straight edge

Masking tape

oil-based paint you should also be aware that some contain lead which is toxic if ingested, so you need to be careful when using certain oils on furniture or other items that will be used by children.

There are several types of specialist paints used in this book which are described below.

Acrylic paints

These are sold in jars and tubes and can be mixed with water, but using an acrylic medium will keep the colours stronger. They are very quick-drying – make sure that you do not allow the paint to dry on the brushes, or you will not be able to wash it off.

Cold ceramic paints

These are for decorative (not utilitarian) use. There are specially-formulated ranges of paints for applying in a range of colours and can, of course, be mixed with one another to make up other colours. (See also Solvent- and Water-based ceramic paints, to the right.)

Enamel paints

Lead-based paints giving a smooth, hard surface covering. Commonly sold in art, craft and modelling shops, they are relatively expensive. Their lead content makes them poisonous, and obviously they are dangerous for painting any objects where there is even the slightest possibility that the item will come into contact with your own or another person's mouth. However, lead paint is extremely durable and sold in a far greater variety of shades and colours than that of specialist ceramic paints.

Fabric paints

The popularity of fabric painting has meant that there is a bewilderingly wide variety of textile paints available, a consequence of manufacturers' attempts to develop safer, easy-to-use paints that do not require fiddly steaming or baking to make them permanent. It is strongly recommended that only water-based non-toxic iron-fixable paints, pigments and guttas or outliners are used, and that attention is paid to the manufacturer's instructions before use. Some colours may spread more than others so it is a good idea to test each type on a scrap of fabric before painting.

Gouache paints

Gouache (or designers' gouache) are opaque watercolour paints, easily handled as long as each layer is allowed to dry before applying the next.

Solvent-based ceramic paints

These are available in the widest colour range, and can be bought with a clear glaze to 'varnish' the finished decoration, which to some extent will protect your work and add to its longevity. Solvent-based paints dry within about 24 hours of application, and can be diluted with white (mineral) spirit. Cold ceramic paints can also be used to decorate unglazed china and biscuitware, but a special undercoat filler must be applied first to seal the porous surface of the china so that it does not over-absorb the colours.

Water-based ceramic paints

These have a brighter finish than their solvent-based equivalents, but come in a smaller range of colours. They can be diluted with water, and dry in about 4 hours. After about 24 hours, they should be hardened off in the oven as this significantly improves the durability of the decoration. Pre-heat the oven to 200°C (400°F, gas mark 6) and wait for 15 minutes if it is an electric oven, 7 minutes if gas. Place the ceramics in the oven and reduce the heat to 150°C (300°F, gas mark 2). Bake for about 30 minutes, then remove from the oven. Before baking for the first time, it is worth painting a spare ceramic tile and testing it in the oven, since various hazards should be avoided: if the temperature is too high or the ceramics are left for too long in the oven, then colours may take on a brown tinge; if the temperature is too low or the baking time is too short, however, the coloured paint will not harden; and if the paint has not been allowed to dry thoroughly before baking, the paint may blister.

Paint palette

Acrylic paints

Gouache paint

Enamel

Fabric paint

Paintbrushes

Used for applying paint to the surface of the object being decorated. You will need a good range of sizes from fine (for applying detail) to broad (for large washes of colour). Paintbrushes made from sable are the best, but they are expensive; unless you are decorating something special, they are probably not worth the extra expense. If you are just starting out, squirrel brushes are also a natural hair brush but less expensive. Synthetic brushes are the least expensive. Nylon bristle is the most common synthetic, but should not be used with oil-based paints, varnishes or cleaned in solvent such as white (mineral) spirit or turpentine, because the bristles can melt. A new synthetic which is highly recommended is called 'sabelette'. This is an excellent alternative to a natural hair brush as it has the responsiveness and resilience of a sable brush without the accompanying price-tag.

Paintbrushes will last longer and respond better if they are cleaned and cared for. If you are using a water-based acrylic or emulsion, you should wash the brush in warm soapy water directly after use, as water-based paints dry quickly. When an oil-based paint or varnish is used, the brush should be soaked in white (mineral) spirit or turpentine, and then rinsed in water. Also, carefully clean the brush each time you change paint as any traces of the previous colour left in the bristles will leave streaks in the new colour application. To check, blot the washed brush on a piece of kitchen towel (paper towel) before using.

Artist's detail brushes

These come in a range of sizes and are primarily for creating finer details and lines. Most come to a point at the end for precision and accuracy, although brushes with a flat, angled end are also in the artist's detail range, and are particularly good for providing extra control when working along edges or curves.

Filbert brushes

Thick and soft with an oval tip, they are excellent for filling in decorative designs, and creating full, sweeping detail strokes. They work best when well loaded with paint.

Household brushes

These range from approximately 2.5 cm (1 in) up to 10 or 12 cm (4 or 5 in). They are generally used for covering large areas quickly and smoothly. For most furniture projects, a 2.5, 4 or 5 cm (1, 1½ or 2 in) brush will be sufficient.

Stencil brushes

These are tubular with a flat end, and have a short, fat handle that can be gripped from the top for better control. They range anywhere from 1 to 5 cm (½ to 2 in) across. Although you can use a standard brush stroke, stencilling brushes have long, stiff bristles that are better employed over a stencil for instance, by using a dabbing motion. (See stencilling techniques on page 15.)

Stippling brushes

These are rectangular with a grip-like handle and can be used both to apply and lift off paint, creating a variety of textural effects.

Paint palette

An old saucer will serve the purpose, but you can also buy small, plastic rectangular trays, divided into four or five sections. For much of the time, you may be able to use paint directly from the jar, but a palette will come in useful either if you want to mix a small quantity of colour, or if sponging paint onto a surface. You will then be able to control much more easily the amount of paint taken up onto the sponge or tissue.

Pencil

Pencils are available with a range of leads, from hard to smooth. For marking ceramic surfaces, you will need a soft lead (ideally 2B), which will leave easily visible marks. However, when transferring a design using carbon paper, a

Ceramic paint

Stencil brush

Artist's brushes

Stippling brush

Rabbit-skin size

Stencil paper

Sponge

Scalpel

hard lead (H or 2H) is more suitable, since the lead will wear down less quickly and the marks transferred will be finer and more accurate.

Petroleum jelly

This is used as a release agent on a mould from which you want to remove a papier mâché shape once it is dry, and for the gilding projects in this book.

PVA wood glue

Polyvinyl acetate woodworking glue (or white glue) is used to glue paper pieces and cardboard together. When diluted with water, this adhesive can also be used as a sealant for porous surfaces.

Rabbit-skin size granules

Rabbit-skin size is used to produce the solution for gesso, putty, clay colours and gilding water.

Sandpaper

'Wet or dry' sandpaper is best for use on pieces of furniture or other objects to be decorated, and can be used either with water or dry. When used with a little water, the paper gives you an extra smooth, satin finish. Different grades are available and determine the coarseness of the grain. You will only need medium paper for smoothing coarse, bare wood and for using after a filler. Silicone carbide sandpaper is good for sharpening gilding knives, and for sanding down between coats of paint or varnish.

Scalpel (x-acto knife)

A small, light knife shaped so that it can be held much as you would a pen, thus allowing you to cut materials very accurately. The sharp, fine blades are disposable; when one becomes blunt, only it needs replacing. Blades are sold in a variety of shapes, but the best for the purpose of the projects in this book are short and triangular in profile, with a sharp point.

Sponge

The absorbency and texture of sponge make it an ideal material with which to achieve interesting paint effects, since unlike a paintbrush it will not give an even covering.

Stain

Stain, like paint, is available either water-soluble or oil-based. Oil stains tend to be more transparent, but must be left overnight to dry. You can choose a wood stain that will give a light wood the illusion of being a richer, dark wood, or a stain to match a particular colour.

Stencil paper

This is manila paper waterproofed with linseed oil, and it is available in a range of thicknesses (gauges) from art shops. The finer the gauge of stencil paper, the easier it is to cut, and although the thicker gauges are more durable they are only really necessary if you intend to repeat your stencil design a large number of times. If you are unable to buy stencil paper, you could use acetate, but it is more expensive and more difficult to cut. Nevertheless, it is useful if you are stencilling a repeat, as you can see through the film to gauge the distance between patterns.

Whatever your choice, cut the stencil on a plastic cutting mat with a craft knife. Remember to cut away from you, and mind your fingers! You can also buy pre-cut stainless steel stencils in various designs from specialist shops.

Sandpapers

Tracing
paper

PVA
glue

Wood
stain

Tracing paper

By tracing the original design onto tracing paper, it can be transferred onto other objects by using the tracing paper in combination with carbon paper (see left, and Basic Techniques, page 12). The best tracing paper is sold in art and specialist shops, and is usually called artist's tracing paper.

Turpentine

A pungent liquid made from the distilled resin of certain coniferous trees. Turpentine is used in the manufacture of some paints and varnishes and it can be used to thin down the consistency of turpentine-based products. It is also useful for cleaning paintbrushes after use or before you start painting in a different colour, and for cleaning areas of ceramic where paint has accidentally spilt.

Varnishes and waxes

After you have finished painting and decorating a piece of furniture, you will want to seal and protect it from chipping, scratching and general wear. The two general choices are either a varnish or a wax, although you can also use a clear gesso to seal and protect.

Varnishes are available in either matt, satin or gloss finishes. This is a personal choice, matt being a soft, flat finish; satin, soft as well, but with a slight sheen; and gloss bringing a high shine to the finish. You will generally need more than one coat, and you must sand between each coat. A fine steel wool works well with varnishes.

When applying varnish, use a standard household paintbrush. Paint with smooth even strokes, in one direction, and avoid letting varnish drip or accumulate around the edges and any mouldings there might be.

Wax is available in a standard beeswax, or in a variety of other finishes which will slightly change the pallor of your piece. Wax should be applied to thoroughly dried paint with a soft cloth. The first coat should be rather thick and left to dry for a few hours before rubbing off. The second and successive coats can be thinner, and rubbed down after less time. When applying and rubbing down wax, always use small circular movements, using a moderate pressure.

Wallpaper paste

For the papier mâché projects in this book, cellulose cold water paste is used to paste the layers of paper pieces together. Most proprietary brands contain fungicide, and are therefore unsuitable for use by children. Non-toxic paste powder, for example, is available from educational suppliers, craft shops and some specialist decorating outlets. Mix up according to the instructions on the packet. For additional strength you can add a little PVA adhesive, and some brands now include it in the mix. Cover the paste bowl when not in use with an air-tight lid or damp cloth. Wrap up unwanted paste in newspaper and always throw it away – do not wash it down the drain.

A rather messy alternative, which has a short life, is a flour and water paste, but this is best avoided unless it is your only option.

White (mineral) spirit

This spirit is used both for cleaning purposes (brushes and any surfaces that have received unwanted paint), and to thin oil-based paints.

Basic Techniques

All of the major techniques used in this book are covered in this section, so whether you would like to know how to mask an object or prepare furniture, you need look no further.

Working out your design

You should always work out your design on paper first, and in most instances it will be necessary to have the object you want to decorate in front of you. As accurately as possible, draw its shape onto the paper to its actual size – since most objects are three-dimensional, you will have to imagine a cross-section drawn through the middle. You can now start drawing in the design you want to paint. As you draw, think about the various components of your design and the most sensible order in which to transfer them to the object. If the design is floral, for example, it will be most sensible either to draw in stems first, and then to fit in the flowers and leaves around them, or else to drop the flower shapes at intervals around the body of the object and then fill in the leaves and stems. Similarly, think about the order of painting - if you are not very skilled with a paintbrush, then try to restrict yourself to as few colours as possible and to broad areas of colour. When you have a finished design on paper, it is probably worth annotating it, or making notes to remind yourself of the order of work involved in transferring the design to the object and painting in the various elements.

Depending on how formal the design is, you may also have to work out on paper separate elements such as a border design. This may involve drawing out an overhead view of the rim of a pot, say, or measuring the circumference of the pot and drawing it out flat as a long, thin rectangle. By reading through a selection of the projects in this book, you should gain a good idea of the various pitfalls and the stages involved.

Resizing a design

If you want to trace off any of the designs in this book and then transfer them to the object to be painted, you will first have to resize them. For all of the projects in this book, this will involve enlarging the design to the correct dimensions, but you can equally use the process in reverse to reduce the size of a design.

Probably the simplest method is to use the enlargement and reduction facility on a photocopying machine, which will make sure that the design is

To enlarge or reduce, draw one grid over your tracing, and make another for the new size.

faithfully reproduced. However, most machines only enlarge up to 156% of the original size, so you would have to use the machine twice if you wanted to double the size of the design. This method also depends, of course, on your having access to a photocopier with this facility, although an increasing number of shops now offer a photocopying service.

The traditional method is not difficult for most designs, although accuracy is important and you may have problems if the design is very intricate. The technique consists of drawing a grid of squares over the original design and then copying the design, square for square, onto a larger (or smaller, if you want to reduce the size) grid. First, trace the design from the book centrally onto a piece of tracing paper, transfer it onto a piece of paper and draw a grid of squares over it. On a second piece of paper, draw out a square or rectangle to the size you want the finished design and then draw in a grid of the same number of squares as are on the traced design, but larger or smaller in size (depending on whether you want to enlarge or reduce the size of the design). Mark on the second grid the equivalent points at which the original design bisects a line on the grid you drew over it, then draw in the design on the new grid, square by square, checking it carefully against the original

For example, if you wanted to double the size of a design for one of the projects in this book, you could overlay a grid of 2.5 x 2.5 cm (1 x 1 in) squares on the original and then draw up a second grid of 5 x 5 cm (2 x 2 in) squares and then proceed as above; if you wanted to make the design half its original size, then you would simply draw a second grid of 1.2 x 1.2 cm ($^1/_2$ x $^1/_2$in) squares. The important thing is to have the same number of squares on both grids.

Transferring a design

Trace the design accurately onto a piece of tracing paper cut to a size so that there is a generous margin around the design. Cut a piece of carbon paper to roughly the same size as the piece of

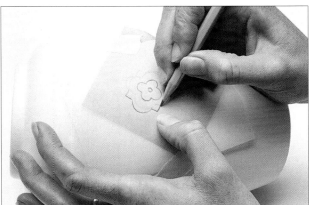

Above: The first stage in transferring a design it to trace off the reference material.

Left: Transfer the design onto the ceramic using carbon paper.

tracing paper, and position the carbon paper, carbon-side down, on the area of the object onto which you want to transfer the design. Place the piece of tracing paper on top of the piece of carbon paper, and stick it temporarily in place with a small piece of masking tape (this makes sure that the paper does not slip while you are transferring the design). Now, simply draw over the traced line of the design, pressing hard with the tip of a pencil so that the carbon paper transfers the motif onto the ceramic surface.

By slightly altering the position of the carbon paper in relation to the tracing paper, you can use the same piece of paper to transfer the design as many times as you require onto the ceramic object.

Templates

Templates are guides used to trace around in order to transfer a design or image onto a piece of furniture for painting. By using them to transfer a series of images, you can create many different types of patterns. Two different techniques for making templates are used in the decorated furniture projects in this book; one using thin paper cardboard, and one using birchfaced plywood.

Bold shapes, and objects which are the same on both sides when divided in half, such as flowers and leaves, make the best sources for templates. You may wish to draw your idea on paper first, then paste the drawing directly onto folded cardboard or plywood. The drawing can then be used as a guide to

cut around. It may also be helpful to measure the surface that you wish to paint, and then make a quick rough sketch of your design to see how each trace of the template will fit into the overall decoration. It's not even necessary to draw the actual design; you can substitute simple block shapes to the approximate size of your template. If you do this before you make your template, you will be able to use it to determine the exact size that the template needs to be so that each trace fits correctly into the decorative pattern. If you find that the actual image that you have chosen is too large or too small to make the appropriately-sized template for your piece of furniture, and you feel uncomfortable trying to redraw it larger or smaller, enlarge or reduce as described to the left.

Masking-out on ceramics

It is often useful to mask-out an area or areas of the object you are decorating in order to prevent paint from covering part of the surface. There are a variety of techniques you can use to achieve this, depending on the paint technique you are applying. Stencils are used not so much to mask out the blank area as to paint in a repeat motif represented by the outline of the stencil; masking paper, masking tape and masking fluid, on the other hand, all allow you to paint with less care than would otherwise be necessary by protecting chosen parts of the object from paint.

Stencils

Depending on the number of times you plan to use your stencil design, you can cut stencils from watercolour paper, which is relatively durable; however, special stencil board or acetate are harder-wearing and give cleaner, more definite lines (see Materials and Equipment, page 10). For details on cutting out a stencil see Making stencils on page 15.

Masking paper

Cut the paper out using a scalpel (x-acto knife). Again, consider buying a special cutting board from an art shop.

Use a ruler when cutting masking tape to ensure perfectly straight lines.

The upper surface of masking paper is difficult to mark, but you can mark the shape you want to cut out in one of two ways: mark the backing paper (which is later peeled away), bearing in mind that what you mark should be the mirror-image of the shape you want to stick down; or else mark the shape onto a piece of tracing paper and stick this down on top of the masking paper, cutting through both surfaces to leave the required design. Masking paper is very easily cut, so be careful not to rush the job. If you are cutting straight lines then it is easiest to use a ruler, ideally with a metal edge. Always hold the ruler so that the scalpel (x-acto knife) blade is on the waste side of the masking paper, so that if the blade slips you will not have to start all over again.

When you have cut out the required shape or shapes, work out their rough position on the object, then peel away the backing paper and stick down the masking paper firmly in place. Wipe over it with a soft cloth to remove any air bubbles, then run a finger nail around the edge of the masking paper to make sure that it is securely fixed.

Masking tape

If you want a hard painted edge around the border of, say, a mug, vase or piece of furniture, then the simplest way to achieve this is by using masking tape. Simply mark at intervals the depth of the border or the width of the stripe and then carefully stick down the masking tape, aligning it with the marks. Run a finger nail around the edge of the tape to make sure that it is stuck firmly in place and then start painting.

Although masking tape allows you to paint with less care than would otherwise be necessary, you should not abandon all caution. Apply the paint so that the sweeps of your brush follow the line of the tape rather than being perpendicular to it. Do not wait for the paint to dry thoroughly before removing the tape, but allow it to dry to a sticky consistency. If necessary, wipe away any paint that has seeped underneath the masking tape.

Masking fluid

This is most commonly used for watercolour painting and allows you to mask out areas by applying the liquid to the objects with a paintbrush. Masking fluid should be used quite thickly, and is simply applied with a brush as if it were paint. Its great advantage is that it is so easily applied and allows you to mask out areas that would otherwise be too intricate. Simply apply the fluid to follow the shape(s) you want to mask out, wait for it to dry and then apply paint to the area you do want to cover, painting over the masking fluid as well. Whereas with the other masking-out techniques you should only wait for the paint to dry to a tacky consistency, with masking fluid you should wait for the paint to dry

Carefully apply masking fluid onto the surface to create the shape you wish to be masked. Then leave it until the fluid has dried.

thoroughly. At this stage, simply pierce the dry masking fluid with the tip of the scalpel (x-acto knife) and pull it up and away from the ceramic. The rubber latex base of the fluid means that it is quite stretchy, and you may have to ease it off at the edges as you pull it away. When the masking fluid has been removed, clean up the edges with the blade to make sure you have a hard finished line. Always make sure that you wash your hands thoroughly immediately after using masking fluid.

Painting

With a paintbrush

The two most important rules when applying paint with a paintbrush are first to match the size of the paintbrush to the surface area you are covering (see Materials and Equipment, page 9) and second not to take up too much paint onto your brush at any one time. Use a thick brush for covering large areas, a fine one for detail work and try to keep your brush strokes regular and following the same basic direction, whether up and down or left to right.

Ceramic paints are quite thick, but they can be diluted using water or white (mineral) spirit (depending on whether they are water-based or solvent-based); however, if you are using them for the first time, it is worth experimenting a little first, either on a piece of paper, or ideally, on a ceramic surface such as a spare tile.

Paint over the area to be coloured (and the masking fluid as well); then pull off the dry masking fluid with a scalpel (x-acto knife).

With a sponge

This will give you a dappled covering of paint and the finished look will depend upon how much paint you take up onto the sponge and the density of the sponge itself: a large, open sponge will give a broad covering, whereas a finer sponge will give a closer finish. You can also achieve a sponged look using tissue paper screwed up into a loose ball – again, the more tightly you twist the paper, the closer the finished appearance.

Stencilling

Stencilling is a traditional decorative technique which uses a shape cut from clear acetate film or paper stencil cardboard. The stencil is then positioned on the object to be decorated, and thick paint is applied through the stencil with a sponge or stencilling brush. Fabric pens are also very effective for this technique on textiles.

Stencilling is very versatile and may be used to make random or repeat patterns. It looks particularly effective when used in conjunction with other techniques, such as sponging, or when embellished with metallic outliners. It is an ideal method for decorating walls and furniture or anything that requires a fairly large repeat, such as bedlinen.

With a stipple brush

Stippling is a painting technique used to create a soft, grainy, textural effect by using the tip of a brush and patting or dabbing it over a wet coat of paint (or dry if stencilling). Any brush with coarse bristles and a wide base can be used, although special stippling brushes produce the best effect. An excellent tip for achieving a good stippling effect is to work from a small plate, squeezing out only a small amount of paint at a time, and dabbing the brush into the paint. The most common mistake experienced when stippling is having far too much paint on the brush. If this happens, blot the brush on a piece of kitchen towel (paper towel) to remove the excess. Check that paint has not spread onto the back of the stencil before placing the stencil on the next area you wish to decorate.

Making stencils

Cut a piece of stencil board to a size slightly larger than your motif, then transfer the motif centrally to the board using tracing paper and carbon paper (see above). You will need to hold the stencil on a hard, flat surface when you are cutting it out. Remember that the cutting surface will be scratched as you cut, so either buy a purpose-made cutting board or mat from an art shop or use a scrap piece of melamine (wood will quickly blunt scalpel [x-acto knife] blades and will also make accurate cutting difficult). Hold the stencil board steady and start cutting at one corner of the motif, drawing the blade in the direction of your cutting arm, away from your spare hand. As it becomes necessary, rotate the stencil board so that you can continue cutting with a relatively fluid movement. Always try to avoid breaking the sweep of your knife in the middle of a line, as this will probably result in a slight nick in the outline of the motif. Begin with the smaller elements in your design, as once the larger ones have been cut out you will lose some of the rigidity of your material and it could rip slightly at the edges. This is particularly true of acetate.

Preparing furniture for painting

Unfinished wood

When you buy an unfinished piece of furniture that is ready to paint, check first that it has not been coated in a sealing wax to protect the wood. If it has, this must be removed before you can begin painting. This is easily done by rubbing with white (mineral) spirit which will dissolve the wax, and then follow by sanding with fine-grade sandpaper. If the piece is unwaxed, wipe down with a damp cloth or white (mineral) spirit and follow with a light sanding to remove any roughness. Do not use a wet cloth, as water will sink into the grain and could warp the piece. The piece is now ready to be undercoated as for old wood.

Old wood

Good condition: older pieces of furniture take more preparation and consideration than new ones. If the piece is in good condition, and the paint or finish is still relatively unmarred, you can give the entire piece one or two good coats of gesso (see Materials and Equipment, page 8). This works as a sealant and creates a smooth surface to work on. Be sure that you lightly sand over the entire piece after each coat has dried with either a fine-grade sandpaper, or wire wool.

Poor condition: if the piece is not in good condition, it will need to be completely stripped of any existing wax, paint or varnish. The best way to do this is by dissolving the old finish with a liquid stripper, which can be bought in

Stencils can be cut from either clear acetate, or from stencil board or card, as shown here.

Sand thoroughly before painting and between coats.

most paint and hardware stores. Follow the directions given as each brand will be slightly different. It may take several applications of the stripping agent to get down to the bare wood. It is a good idea to use protective gloves and a mask while working with solvents.

Filling: you will want to have the smoothest surface possible to paint on. If the piece has any gashes or deep scars, you can buy an all-purpose wood filler which can be applied, and when dry, sanded smooth with the rest of the piece. Follow the instructions for the particular product that you buy.

Woodworm: if you are using an old piece of furniture, check carefully for woodworm. This will manifest itself in the form of tiny holes in the wood. If you do not take care of this, it will eventually weaken the piece irrevocably and can also spread to other pieces of wooden furniture in the house and to wood floors. You can buy wood de-worming product at most hardware and paint stores; it will come in a can with a long, thin, tubular applicator, and needs to be injected into every hole. Do this systematically so that you don't miss any holes.

Sanding: it is important to sand before painting, and between every coat of paint or varnish that you apply (see Materials and Equipment, page 10). Steel or wire wool can be used for smoothing mouldings, rounded legs, and other areas that are difficult to treat with stiff sandpaper. For flat surfaces, it is helpful to wrap your sandpaper around a small block of wood. This will allow you to apply even pressure to all areas. Most importantly, when sanding, remember to sand following the direction of the grain of the wood.

Papier mâché

When you start on a project, make sure that you have everything you need, and, ideally, find a worksurface where you can leave everything without having to clear up between the various stages of the work.

Tearing up the newspaper

Tear up a generous quantity of newspaper into strips, varying in size according to the shape you are making. You will find that it is much easier to tear in one direction than the other. This is caused by the direction of the grain of the paper, which is determined by the way the sheet passed through the machine during manufacture and the direction of the paper fibres. In most newspapers the grain runs from top to bottom. Tearing the paper gives a feathered edge and produces a smoother finish to the papier mâché than you would achieve by using pieces cut with scissors.

Assembly/preparing the mould

If you are using a mould from which you will remove the papier mâché shape, give it a generous coating of petroleum jelly before applying the first layers of pasted paper. This will prevent the paper from sticking to the shape. If you are making a mould from modelling plastic, it is not necessary to use petroleum jelly for small shapes as the material has a certain amount of grease in it. However, it is advisable to use it for more complicated shapes to avoid any possibility of sticking.

Pasting and applying the newspaper

Use your hand to smear paste onto one or both sides of the paper strip, and squeeze off the excess with your fingers. You can allow the paste to soak in for a few minutes if you like, placing the pieces around the edge of the bowl before applying. This is advisable if you are using poor quality newspaper, to allow time for absorption of the paste.

The total number of layers you apply will depend on both the size of the object and the strength required for the piece you are making. If you are covering a small cardboard template (for a piece of jewellery, for instance) you will need to use only two layers of newspaper; for a bowl that is going to be used to carry fruit you should use at least eight layers. When you have completed a layer, smooth over it with your fingers to remove any bubbles and excess glue.

Drying time

The amount of time required to dry the pasted paper obviously varies according to the temperature of your room and the weather. The drying times recommended for the various stages of the papier mâché projects in this book are based on working in a mild, temperate climate, so you will have to adjust the estimates depending on your own conditions. Using a warm airing cupboard will speed up the drying time.

If you dry the piece layer by layer, you will have a good idea of drying rates. If you apply all the layers in one session, test to see how dry the piece is after two or three days. If working on a mould, prize away the sides with a blunt knife and check to see if the paper comes away easily. If it does not, allow to dry for a further day. Once out of the mould, allow an extra day's drying time so that the side that has been in contact with the mould is completely dried out.

Drying should be done at an even temperature. This is important if you are using a balloon as a mould. Any dramatic changes in temperature, or extreme heat, may cause the balloon to burst or to shrivel up.

Finishing the shape

If you are trimming the edges (for the mirror or bowl project, for instance), you should 'bind' the cut edge with small strips of pasted paper and allow to dry.

Chapter

1

Living Rooms

Decorative paint techniques need not be confined to the walls of your living room. Paint the fireplace tiles or decorate a vase in colours to complement their surrounds, or add some inventive touches to cushions and cupboards.

In this section there are nine beautifully photographed projects, each designed to add a touch of originality to your living room. The techniques are varied, so whatever your taste, you will find something to please.

Sponged Tea Service

By Lesley Harle

A colourful tea service such as this can make a fine decorative display in a kitchen or living room. (Cold ceramic paints are decorative and not utilitarian: if any of the items are likely to be put to use, you must not apply paint to any area that will come into contact with the mouth unless the item is fired; see page 3.) The elements of the design can be used in a variety of permutations to decorate each piece individually if you want. At its simplest, you can use just the sponging technique to brighten up a dull teapot. At the other extreme, you could extend the range of decorated items to plates, and you could even use enamel paints to decorate a tray to match.

Preparation and tips

● Use water-based ceramic paints which are then baked in the oven for greater durability.

● Use sponging for the saucer, sponging and scallop shapes for the sugar bowl, feathers for the milk jug etc. Depending on the proportions of your service, it may be necessary to scale down the size of the motifs before applying them to objects smaller than the teapot.

● Do not apply the scalloped border to the teapot if you intend to serve tea from it, or paint to the edge of the tea cups. Remove the lid from the teapot and measure 3 cm (1½ in) around the rim of the body, marking this at intervals all the way around with a fine black marker pen. Cut a strip of masking paper in a long curve, remove the backing, and stick the bottom edge of the masking paper along the line of dots.

Materials and equipment

Tea service

Ruler

Marker pen

Masking paper

Sponge or tissue paper

Scrap paper

Paintbrushes

Cold ceramic paints

Compass

Pencil

Tracing paper

Protractor

Turpentine

Carbon paper

▼ **1** Sponge on the yellow paint to the body of the teapot using a sponge or, better still, tissue paper. Screw up the tissue paper, dip it in to the yellow paint, and take off the excess by dabbing it onto a piece of scrap paper. In this way you will get the paint to the density you want. Sponge onto the body of the pot until it is covered, working carefully around the edge of the spout, which remains unpainted, paint the knob on the lid of the teapot yellow. Allow the yellow paint to dry thoroughly before removing the masking paper.

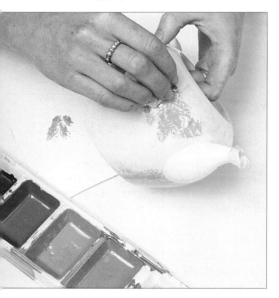

▲ **3** If you intend using the teapot, you should not apply the scalloped border, but leave it unpainted instead – miss out steps 3-6 inclusive.

The scalloped border requires time and patience if it is going to look good. Measure the diameter at the top of the body of the teapot; halve this to find the radius, and set your compass to this measure. Draw the appropriate circle on a piece of tracing paper. Draw another circle, concentric with the first, but with a radius 3 cm (1½ in) larger – the space between the two circles represents the border at the top of the tea pot. The border of the pot is decorated with nine scallop shapes, so you need to divide the 360° circle into nine 40° 'slices' using a protractor. The area between the two circles and the outward-radiating lines is the space available for the scallop shape, which you can now draw in.

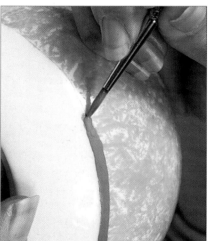

▲ **2** Remove the masking paper from around the edge of the border, and use the top edge of the yellow paint as a guide to paint in a thin green line.

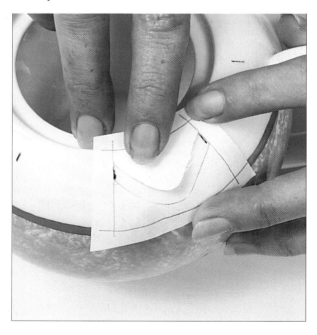

◀ **4** Trace one of the scallop shapes onto a piece of masking paper, and very carefully cut it out. Do not remove the backing paper, but instead use the section of masking paper with the scallop cut away as a template to mark off the position for the scallops around the border of the teapot. Use a fine black pen to mark the points where the scallops join up with one another.

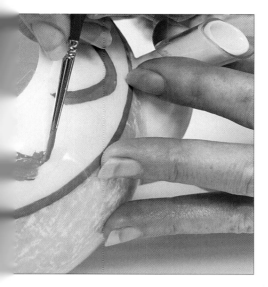

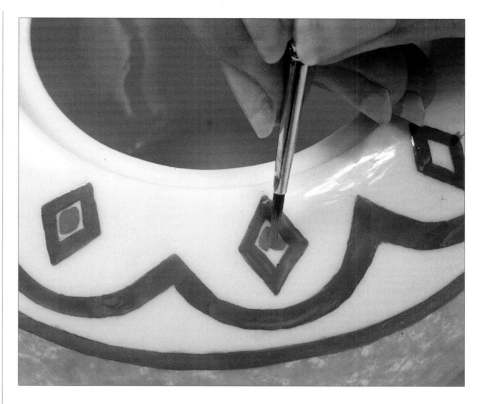

△ 5 Cut a further eight pieces of masking paper with the scallop shapes traced on and then cut out. These are used to mask out the rest of the border area while you paint in the scallops. The scallops are painted in one by one, and you will need a clean piece of masking paper for each. Remove the backing from one of the pieces of masking paper and stick it down, aligning the ends of the scallop shape with the marks you have penned in. Paint in the scallop shape in green.

Repeat the process, working your way around the border, but only painting every other scallop shape, since otherwise the stuck-down masking paper will smudge the scallop you have just painted. Wait for the paint to dry before painting the remaining scallops - if, as here, you have nine scallop shapes, then you will still have to wait a second time before you can paint in the final scallop. If the paint should seep underneath the masking paper, remove the excess using a fine paintbrush dipped in turpentine.

△ 6 Return to your plan of the teapot border (the two circles with the scallops drawn in) and draw a diamond shape the appropriate size to fit between the scallops and the top of the border. Trace the diamond shape onto a piece of tracing paper, and transfer it around the border using a piece of carbon paper. Outline the diamonds in green paint and leave to dry before filling them in with an ochre yellow.

◀ 7 To complete the teapot, draw a feather shape onto a piece of paper, and then transfer it to the yellow body of the pot using tracing paper and carbon paper. Apply the shape more or less randomly, rotating it through different angles. Carefully paint in the feathers using one or more colours and wait to dry.

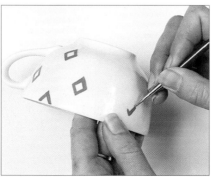

◀ 8 The cup is decorated only with the diamond shapes from the teapot border. Transfer the shape as above, paying particularly attention to spacing.

Begin with a diamond shape applied to the middle of the front of the cup – this gives you a point from which to calculate the position of the other diamonds. Calculate the spacing accurately (see Striped mug, page 54), or transfer a central row of diamond shapes and then fill in the rows above and below in the gaps.

Floral Vase

By Lesley Harle

Blue-and-white painted ceramics have always been popular, perhaps the most famous being the willow pattern. The freehand design shown here updates a familiar theme, and can be as simple as you want it to be – even with just the trefoils applied, the vase already looks very attractive. This design acknowledges the fact that many people may find it difficult to paint accurately on a curved surface, and so makes a virtue of not following strictly the outlines of the trefoils, stems and leaves.

Materials and equipment

Vase

Cold ceramic paints

Paintbrushes

Pencil

Carbon paper

Tracing paper

Masking tape

Preparation and tips

● The first element of the design to be applied is that of the trefoils. The shape you want to apply should correspond to the main part of the trefoil, and should not include the darkest blue outline, which is applied freehand at the end.

● You can either draw the trefoils freehand, or you can trace off the shape from the illustration reproduced here. Look at the photograph of the finished project to get an idea about the spacing; the trefoils need to be spaced fairly regularly to achieve a balanced look.

● You will also see that the trefoils form approximate columns, running up the vase, and that they are spaced roughly mid-way between the trefoils above and below them, so that you could almost draw up an interconnecting grid of triangles. Bear in mind also that you must leave sufficient space between the trefoils to allow for the stems and leaves to be added. If you think you have pencilled in too few or too many trefoils you will probably have to begin applying them again from scratch – the pencil marks can be simply wiped off using a damp cloth.

▲ **1** Paint in the blue that forms the outer band of colour (not the thin outline of darkest blue) and leave to dry. Paint in the yellow details: draw the brush in three petal-shaped sweeps, so that the middle of each 'petal' is left white, giving the appearance of seeds. At this stage you should also paint the rim at the top of the vase, again in yellow. Take care to try and achieve a neat finishing line between the rim and the body of the vase.

▲ **2** Make sure that the paint is thoroughly dry before proceeding, otherwise you might end up with fingerprints smudging the trefoils. Next, draw in the stems that curve between the trefoils. Try to achieve a series of main stems curving up the body of the vase, with subsidiary stems filling in any large gaps. Pencil in the curves of the stems.

◄ **3** Use the lightest blue to paint in the stems and the leaves. You will need a fine paintbrush for this, and you should try to paint each sweep of the stem as one continuous stroke, since otherwise it may be too obvious at which points you started applying a fresh amount of paint. Paint in the leaves with generous sweeps of the brush.

Finally, when the pale blue tint has dried, you can paint in the dark blue outline using a fine paintbrush. The pattern here depends partly for its effect on the hand-painted quality of the finished piece. For this reason, it is not important to follow exactly the lines of the trefoils, stems and leaves; the leaves benefit from the mismatch between the outline and the painted area, contributing to the loose, free quality of the design.

Ornamental Plate

By Lesley Harle

The stunning washed effect on the border of this ornamental plate is more simply achieved than you would think possible. The success of the project depends little on painting skills, since the only freehand work involves the spirals on the quadrilaterals and the wavy border. You could omit these from the design if you do not have the confidence to paint them.

Materials and equipment

Plate

Masking paper

Scalpel (x-acto knife)

Paintbrushes

Cold ceramic paints

Turpentine

Cloth or tissue

Pencil

Preparation   and   tips

● The washed effect is achieved by thinning the ceramic paints with turpentine, a technique that only works with the solvent-based variety. Make sure you buy the correct type of paint.

● The finished plate is purely for decorative use. Although the decoration is durable, it will not withstand repeated washing and on no account should food ever come into contact with ceramic paint diluted with turpentine, unless the item is first fired (see page 3).

● Cut a piece of masking paper to a size that will cover the flat central section of the plate and overlap onto the raised edge. Remove the backing paper and stick the masking paper down onto the middle of the plate. Smooth the masking paper from the middle outwards to remove as many air bubbles as possible.

▼ 1 Using a scalpel (x-acto knife), carefully cut along the line of the curve of the flat oval shape to remove the excess masking paper that obscures the rimmed edge that you are going to paint. Work patiently so that the masking paper you are left with covers the oval area as accurately as possible and so that the cut line follows a smooth curve. Run a finger nail around the edge of the masking paper to seal it in place and so reduce the risk of paint seeping underneath onto the main part of the plate.

Cut the quadrilateral shapes from a piece of masking paper. Although these are not regular, they should all be approximately the same size, since the design will otherwise look unbalanced. If you plan to paint the quadrilaterals in alternate colours as shown, then you must have an even number of them. You do not, of course, have to use quadrilaterals: triangles would look equally good, although shapes with five or more sides are more difficult to paint.

When you have cut out the required number of quadrilaterals – the design shown here uses 14, but the number may vary according to the size of your plate – place them in position around the rim of the plate. Do not remove the backing paper until you are satisfied that they are correctly spaced and that you do not want to change the number of quadrilaterals. When you are happy with the number and spacing, remove the backing paper and stick down the pieces of masking paper in position.

▼ 2 Mix up the colour with which you will paint the background: this aquamarine is a combination of blue and yellow. The washed effect is achieved by applying small quantities of the paint to random areas of the rim, in quite thick brush strokes.

Apply the paint to a couple of places close to one another on the plate, clean the paintbrush in turpentine, and then take a small amount of turpentine onto your brush and spread the paint out from the places you have applied it. Your brush strokes do not need to be at all even, since the effect you want to achieve depends on a random combination of densely and lightly covered areas. Repeat the process until you have worked your way around the whole rim of the plate.

▲ **3** The paint will very quickly dry to a tacky consistency; at this stage, you can remove the pieces of masking paper. Using the edge of the scalpel (x-acto knife), lift the edge of the masking paper and pull it away. If you find that the background colour has seeped under the masked-out areas, dip a piece of clean cloth or tissue in a small amount of turpentine and wipe the excess paint clean. Leave the paint to dry thoroughly.

▲ **4** Paint in the quadrilaterals using exactly the same method as for painting the background. Obviously, you will need to be slightly more careful this time, since you do not want the paint to spill over onto the background colour. Use a finer paintbrush and be sparing with both the amount of paint and the amount of turpentine you use. If you do paint over the background colour, wipe it away immediately using a piece of tissue. If you are right-handed, paint the quadrilaterals working in a clockwise direction, since this will reduce the risk of your hand blotching one of the quadrilaterals you have already painted; if you are left-handed, work in an anti-clockwise direction. Paint every other quadrilateral in one colour first, wait for them to dry and then carefully paint the remaining quadrilaterals in your chosen second colour.

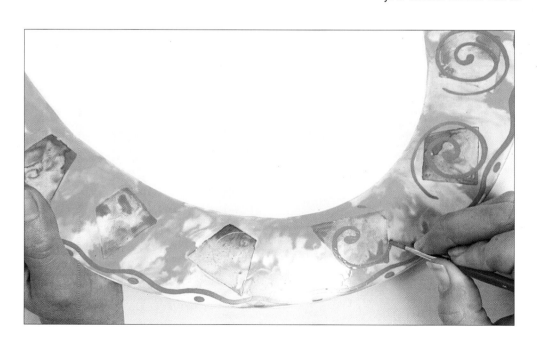

◀ **5** When the paint is thoroughly dry, apply the final touches of decoration. If you are worried about painting the spirals freehand, draw them in first using a pencil. Paint in the wavy border along the outside rim of the plate, adding spots of paint at intervals as shown in the finished photograph. Allow the paint to dry and the plate is then ready to be displayed.

Victorian Fireplace Tiles

By Lesley Harle

The design of these tiles is intended to border a fireplace. However, if you do not have a fireplace or it is unsuitable for tiling, then you could adapt the design, perhaps omitting the border and exaggerating the twists of the stem, for other types of tile. The flower heads on their own could be used as a charming central motif on decorative plates.

Materials and equipment

15 x 15 cm (6 x 6 in) tiles

Tile cutter and scorer

Ruler

Pencil

Tissue paper

Paintbrushes

Masking fluid

Masking paper/masking tape (optional)

Ceramic (or enamel) paints

Scalpel (x-acto knife)

Turpentine

Tracing paper

Carbon paper

Preparation and tips

● If your fireplace is not the height of an exact number of tiles then cut out a tile to the required size to fill the gap. Score a line along the glazed side of the tile and break along this line using a tile cutter. For a neat appearance, place the cut tile at the bottom of the column, where it will be hidden.

● Calculate how many tiles you need for one side of the fireplace and place them all in a row. Number them on the back from one to six, or however many tiles you need.

● Measure 2.5 cm (1 in) in from the edge of both sides of each tile and across the top of the top tile at fairly regular intervals, marking the point with a pencil. Join up the dots using a ruler or straight edge to mark the border. Use the pencil to draw out the wavy line that runs down either side of the border and across the top. For a neat appearance, the lines drawn on either side should be approximate mirror images.

▶ **1** Paint over the pencil wavy lines using a paintbrush dipped in watercolour masking fluid, which you should apply quite thickly. Next apply small circles of masking fluid dotted at intervals between the wavy lines, for the white dots in the design.

◀ **2** When the masking fluid has dried thoroughly, mix the burgundy-coloured paint from about one part blue to two parts red. If you do not want the tile to look hand-painted, apply masking paper or masking tape along the pencilled lines of the border before you start painting, to give a hard finished edge. Apply the burgundy paint to the border, covering the entire area including the masking fluid. Be careful, however, not to paint beyond the pencil line perimeter (or masking tape) and try to apply quite a thin, even coat of paint. As soon as you have done so, apply a second coat of the burgundy colour, but more thickly this time, to give an even covering. Work as quickly as you can without sacrificing accuracy since this should prevent the brush strokes being too obvious to the naked eye.

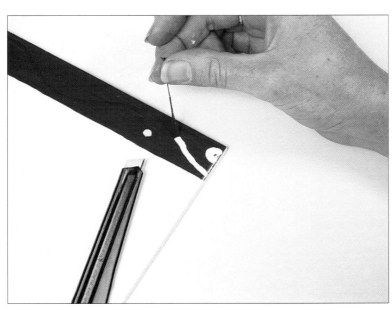

◀ **3** When the burgundy paint has dried, remove the masking fluid using the blade of a scalpel (x-acto knife). Pierce the masking fluid towards the bottom of one of the tiles, and, using the blade of the scalpel (x-acto knife), gently pull it up and away from the tile. Do not worry if it does not all come away in one go, or if it comes away unevenly: any that remains can be scraped away carefully. Use the scalpel (x-acto knife) to tidy the edges of the wavy line when all the masking fluid has been removed. Then dip a paintbrush in turpentine, take off the excess, and run the brush over the white lines to make sure it is clean.

▲ 4 Lay the tiles out in a row again, checking the number on the back to make sure that they are in the correct order and that the border pattern matches up. Using a pencil, draw the sweeping central stem, curving it from one side to the other of the central area.

Draw in the smaller stems, the leaves and the pansies. You may find it easier to draw out the whole design first on a piece of paper and then use tracing paper and carbon paper to transfer it to the tiles (see Basic Techniques, page 12); this will also make sure that the design of the tiles on both sides of the fireplace matches up. If you do not feel capable of drawing any part of the design yourself, you could simply trace it from the photograph at the start of the project, enlarging it to fit the dimensions of your tile.

All of the central design is painted freehand, starting with the lime green stem and the leaves. If you want a flat, even finish you will have to apply two coats of the colour, just as you did with the burgundy border.

▼ 5 Once the lime green has dried, start to apply the darker green, first to the stem and then to the leaves. The technique used to paint the leaves is similar to that on the Ornamental Plate project (pages 25-7): apply the colour to the darkest edge of the leaf, clean your brush, and then take up a small amount of turpentine onto your brush and use it to spread the paint gently across the rest of the dark area of the leaf, grading the colour to give it almost the appearance of a watercolour. This effect can be quite tricky to achieve, since you want the gradation to conform to a specific scheme. Patience is called for, and you may want to experiment with the technique first on a spare tile.

▼ 6 Petals of the pansies are painted in the same way as the dark green of the leaves. Paint the yellow petals first, wait for the paint to dry thoroughly, and then paint the red. A significant part of each petal is solid colour, so be sure to apply enough paint in the first place, otherwise the pansies will look thin and washed out.

When the red paint has dried, apply the black to the middle of each flower. Use a medium-sized paintbrush to fill in the very centre and work around and outwards, pulling the brush in gentle strokes to give the impression of the delicate stamen.

Make sure that the tiles are thoroughly dry before fixing them in place at the sides of the fireplace. It may be a good idea to fix a temporary batten against one edge of the fireplace to make sure that the tiles are set in place exactly plumb. Take care when you come to apply tiling grout to the joints: although the excess can be simply wiped away using a damp sponge, if it is left for too long the grout may take part of your painted decoration with it.

Stencilled Chintz Cushion

By Chris Fox

Stencilling onto fabric allows you to design your own textiles and at the same time opens up endless possiblities for creating an individual look to both soft furnishings and clothes.

This chintz-style cushion cover has been created by stencilling through a paper doiley with spray paint. A cut-out floral motif from another piece of fabric has been bonded to the centre of the lace stencil for added interest. Choose natural fabrics like linen, cotton or calico, but test the paint on a scrap first, as absorbency can vary and you may need to apply two or three coats to achieve the colour required. Once stencilled, the fabric can be made up into a cushion cover in the usual way.

Materials and equipment

Square of fabric

Scrap paper

Masking tape

Paper doiley

Spray adhesive

Spray paint

Wallpaper seam roller

Preparation and tips

● Lay the fabric right side up onto a large sheet of scrap paper. Make sure the paper will protect all the surrounding surfaces from the spray paint mist which will inevitably ensue once you begin. Fix the fabric at each corner with masking tape.
● Place the doiley face down on a sheet of scrap paper and spray with a light coating of adhesive. Allow it to dry for a few seconds.

▼ **1** Turn the doiley over and position it in the centre of the fabric and press down firmly so that no paint will be able to seep underneath. For the best results, use a wallpaper seam roller and apply firm pressure all over.

▲ **2** Spray paint over the cloth, ensuring it covers the doiley and right up to all edges of the fabric. Hold the can about 15 cm (6 in) from the surface and use a gentle pumping action on the button. Move the can slightly and smoothly from side to side to prevent build-up in any one area.

◀ **3** Leave to dry for a few seconds before gently peeling off the doiley. As a finishing touch you can apply a circle of contrasting fabric to the centre of the lacy design using fabric glue or an iron-on bonding web.

Colourwashed Corner Cupboard

By Jane Brossard and Sandra Krivine

Corner cupboards are great space savers, creating extra storage in places where the only other option might be to have a customized cabinet installed. As they are generally constructed very simply and out of wood, applying a decorative paint finish can really brighten them up. The stencilling technique illustrated in this project allows you to create a relatively intricate pattern quite easily yet looks as if it was done professionally.

Preparation and tips

● Prepare the corner cupboard for painting according to the instructions on page 15. When the wood is cleaned and prepared, apply one coat of white emulsion, making sure that all areas are covered.

● When the white basecoat has dried, sand the piece lightly with fine sandpaper or wire wool to create a smooth finish, taking care not to remove patches of paint. Paint the cupboard with pale lemon emulsion. Begin your painting on the centre panel of the door and the side panels, as they will be receiving more decoration later and will have time to dry while you paint the other areas.

● If you decide to make your own stencil, see page 15.

● A hairdryer can be used to speed up the drying process, and to give the piece a bit more aged authenticity.

● A little raw umber oil paint can be rubbed over the crackled area, and then rubbed again with a clean cloth. This helps to define the cracks. If you plan to try this, practise first as it can sometimes prove a bit tricky. When everything has dried, wax with an ordinary beeswax polish.

Materials and equipment

Corner cupboard

1 litre (32 fl oz) undercoat: white

1 litre (32 fl oz) vinyl matt emulsion paints: lemon, blue, turquoise

White emulsion

60 ml (2 fl oz) acrylic paints: peach and gold

Paintbrushes: 4 cm (1½ in) household; artist's detail

Glass jam jar

Masking tape

Ready-made stencil

Stencil brush

2 soft cloths

Matt varnish

Lime wax polish or crackle varnish and 'raw umber' oil paint (optional)

▶ **1** Remove the drawer and give it a coat of base colour. Pale blue was used here. You may also choose to paint the inside edges and inside of the drawer, which you will be able to see when the drawer is opened. To add the striped border around the drawer, place strips of masking tape along each edge, taking care to line them up to the edge as straight as possible. You will be painting two stripes at a time. Take two more pieces of tape and position them parallel to two of the sides, leaving a gap the width that you want the stripe to be. Using a stippling or a detail brush, fill in the space between the pieces of tape.

When the first stripes have dried, remove the tape and repeat the process for the other two sides. It is important that any area that will be taped has dried thoroughly before applying it, otherwise when you remove the tape, the paint may peel off.

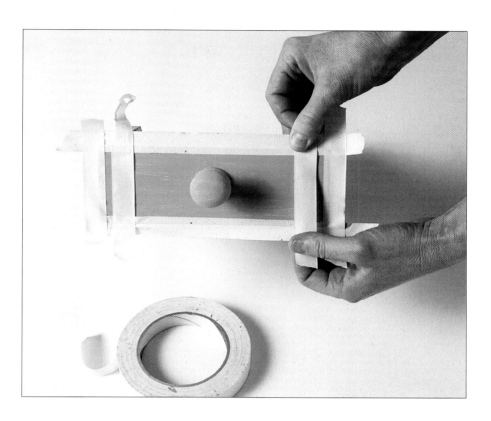

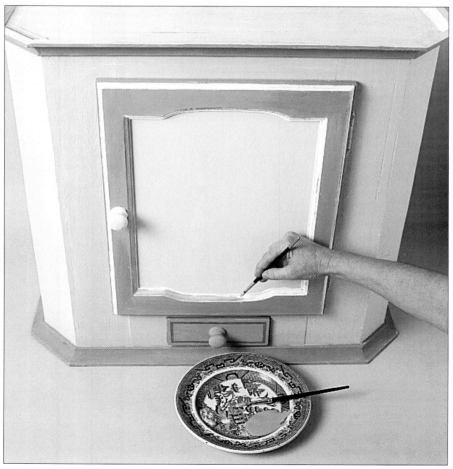

◀ **2** Paint the remainder of the borders and mouldings. Peach, gold and a soft blue were used on this piece. The gold on the inside door moulding creates the look of a picture frame when the stencil decoration is painted onto the door.

▶**3** See-through acetate stencils are created here by placing a sheet of acetate over the image you wish to reproduce, and tracing it onto the sheet with a permanent ink pen. It is then cut out using a stencil knife or a scalpel (x-acto knife). Unlike a template, you do not trace around a stencil and then paint in the design. Paint is applied directly onto the piece of furniture through the acetate using a stencil brush.

Oiled stencil paper or cardboard can be substituted for acetate as you may find it easier to cut. The advantage of acetate though is that you can see through the stencil for a perfect placement of your design.

◀ **4** Position the stencil wherever you wish to paint the design, and stipple the cut-out areas with a stencil brush until you get the intensity of colour that you want. Don't feel that you have to paint within the acetate cut-out, as painting onto the edges will make sure that your image is reproduced clearly. It may help to tape the stencil in place to keep it from moving.

The fruit basket design on the door is reproduced by using one sheet of acetate with a number of different elements, and moving the sheet around to `fill' the basket. The basket itself is stencilled in before the fruit and flowers. Make sure that your design is left to dry completely before the stencil is moved to another place, as the acetate will smear the wet area.

▶ **5** The grape stencil is applied to both of the side panels. This stencil is a Lyn le Grice design. (Lyn le Grice produces a number of stencils that can be bought ready-made.)

▲ **6** When the piece is completely dry, coat the entire cupboard with two coats of varnish, allowing the first to dry thoroughly before applying the second. This piece was then treated with a lime wax polish, which gives it its chalky patina and generally softens all the colours. Two coats were used, the first applied more liberally than the second, and both rubbed off with a soft cloth. It is recommended that you try a small area before waxing the entire piece. A beeswax polish can be used instead if the lime wax finish does not give you the effect that you desire.

◀ **7** Another option for the stencilled area is to use a crackle varnish instead of the lime wax. This produces the effect of ageing, and is applied after the piece has been varnished all over. Each manufacturer will provide instructions with their crackle varnish product.

Papier Mâché Bowl

By Marion Elliot

This decorative bowl is substantial enough to be used to hold fruit. Its shape is classic and symmetrical. Natural designs, which lend themselves well to round forms, have been used for the decoration. The wider rim at the edge of the base gives the bowl balance, both in visual and physical terms.

The lip of the bowl and the rim of the foot and the join between the two pieces are built up with the addition of rolls of pulpy paper. They give the piece a more substantial appearance and imitate ceramic forms.

Preparation and tips

● Before beginning the paper mâché, tear up the newspaper into strips about 2.5 cm (1 in) wide, and as long as one side of the bowl to be covered plus 2.5 cm (1 in) for the overlap.

● Paste the paper strips in a radiating pattern around the bowl, starting at the centre. Apply eight layers in one session. If possible, use newspapers of two different colours to help you to keep track of the number of layers applied.

● Allow to dry for at least two days and then with a blunt knife, prize the paper away from the bowl. If it comes away easily, remove from the mould and allow the paper to dry again for a day, otherwise, leave it for another day before trying again.

● Allow one day to dry after working the rolls for the lip and rim, and also after joining the pieces.

● To make a paper roll, wipe paste on both sides of a strip of newspaper, about 2.5 x 25 cm (1 x 10 in), fold it in half twice and crumple it up, rolling it in your palms. The rolls are fastened in position with pasted strips of newspaper about 1 cm ($^1/_2$ in) wide, torn to the required lengths.

● When joining the bowl and the foot together with PVA wood glue, allow to dry for about two hours.

● Using waterproof ink allows you to make corrections to the outlining details without the danger of muddying the colours, which might occur if you use black gouache. To make a correction, allow the ink to dry and then cover the area with white gouache, or process white. You can then reapply any base colour where necessary, and go over the outline again in black.

Materials and equipment

1 mould for bowl

1 small mould for foot

Petroleum jelly

Cotton wool (cotton balls)

Bowl for paste

Wallpaper paste (mixed)

Newspaper

Blunt knife

Scissors

Sandpaper (medium- and fine-grade)

PVA wood glue

Emulsion paint

Pencil

Gouache paints: turquoise, spectrum red, cadmium yellow, zinc white

Water pot

Paint palette

Indian ink: black

Polyurethane gloss varnish

Paintbrushes: household, artist's

White (mineral) spirit

▲ **1** Using petroleum jelly, cover the insides of both moulds and work it well over the rims. Apply eight layers of paper strips in one session to both bowls, allowing an overlap of about 2.5 cm (1 in) at the rim.

    When complete, tear some paper into smaller pieces to make a final reinforcing band around the inside rims of both bowls to neaten the ends of the strips. Firm the paper down around the rims and make sure that the overlapping edges of paper protrude from the bowl.

▲ **2** After removing from the mould, trim the edges with scissors and then neaten the cut edges with small strips of pasted paper. Work lightly on the surfaces of both bowls with sandpaper to make them smooth. Use medium-grade sandpaper first, and then finish with fine grade.

◄ **3** Make a lip for the bowl and a rim for the foot by building them up with small rolls of newspaper.

    Tuck two of the rolls under the trimmed edge of the bowl and hold them in position with one hand while you stick the end of a long paper strip on the outside of the lip and over the roll. Then tear it off so that it is pasted to the inside of the bowl. Continue working around the rim and then apply a second layer of small strips over the lip. Work the foot rim in the same way.

    Neaten the joining strips with a band of small strips pasted parallel to the rim on the inside and outside of the bowls. Allow to dry for one day.

    Join the pieces together with glue and allow to dry. To give a smooth contour to the join, apply paper rolls as before, pushing the first well into the join, and allowing a slight ridge to form with the second. Cover them with small strips of paper as before, but this time using three layers. Leave the bowl to dry thoroughly for two days.

▲ **4** Remove any remaining petroleum jelly with cotton wool (cotton balls) and white (mineral) spirit if necessary. Then, using a household paintbrush, apply two coats of white emulsion paint allowing drying time between the coats. When dry, draw the design for your decoration on the bowl with a pencil.

▲ **5** Apply the gouache colours in layers using the artist's brushes. Start with the lightest colour and work up to the darkest.

Mix up the yellow, blue and red paints with some white to achieve light tints and paint the areas required.

◄ **6** Allow the first application of paint to dry for at least an hour before adding the darker areas of yellow, blue and red. Allow to dry.

When quite dry, add the outline detail decoration with black waterproof Indian ink and a thin brush. Allow to dry.

Apply three coats of gloss varnish, allowing each coat to dry before applying the next. Wash out all paintbrushes thoroughly using white (mineral) spirit.

Lacquered Mirror Frame

By Dario Arnese

How many times have you stopped to look at a piece of furniture in your home and contemplated moving it or throwing it out altogether? This mirror frame will encourage anyone to take the time to look at a shape and consider the possibilities of transforming a rather mundane object into a striking centrepiece. The combination of water gilding and lacquer adds elegance to this frame and picks out the delicate relief work.

Preparation and tips

● Check to see that the frame does not need any attention before starting. If it needs filling, apply putty or filler and allow to dry for 30 minutes. Smooth down with 240 wet and dry sandpaper.

● Prepare rabbit-skin size by mixing 55 g (2 oz) rabbit-skin size granules with 575 ml (1 pint) cold water in a metal bowl. Set the bowl in a pan of water and bring to the boil. Reduce the heat and stir the solution while it simmers until the granules have melted and the size takes on a syrup-like consistency (5-10 minutes). Leave to cool slightly before using it.

● Prepare the first coat of gesso by adding 1 part prepared rabbit-skin size to 1 part cold water. Sieve in just enough gesso powder to colour the liquid and stir well. When applied the gesso should appear translucent. Heat the liquid over a bain-marie until it is hot, but not boiling. Using a medium bristle brush, apply to the frame and allow to dry overnight.

Materials and equipment

Oval frame

Putty or filler (optional)

240 wet and dry sandpaper

Rabbit-skin size granules

Gesso powder

Paintbrushes: medium bristle; medium synthetic; large synthetic; small bristle

Silicone carbide sandpaper

Yellow clay

Red clay

Dusting brush

Methylated spirit (wood alcohol)

2 books loose leaf gold

Gilder's pad, knife and tip

Petroleum jelly

Cotton wool (cotton balls)

Agate burnisher

Fine steel wool

Eggshell paint: black

Soft rags

Gloss varnish

White (mineral) spirit

Burnt umber oil colour

Clear wax

▲ **2** Make a red clay solution as for the yellow clay, but mix 2 parts prepared rabbit-skin size to 1 part water. Brush on two coats using a medium synthetic brush. Apply this to the highlights of the frame only, trying not to get the clay in the crevices. Allow to dry for 15-20 minutes.

Using silicone carbide sandpaper, sand down the red and yellow clays until they are smooth to the touch. Remove the dust with a dusting brush.

▲ **1** Re-heat the gesso and use the medium bristle brush to apply 6 coats, allowing each coat to dry before applying the next. Allow the final coat to dry for at least 2 hours, then rub down smooth using first 240 wet and dry sandpaper and then silicone carbide to finish off.

Then make the yellow clay solution. Mix 1 part prepared rabbit-skin size with 1 part water in a metal container in a bain-marie. Once the size has melted, add just enough yellow clay to produce a mixture with the consistency of thick cream. Brush on two coats of yellow clay using a medium bristle brush. Cover the gesso completely, leaving no trace of it showing through.

▲ **3** Make gilding water by filling a container half-full of cold water and slowly adding methylated spirit (wood alcohol) until the water starts to change colour. Heat up some rabbit-skin size and add a teaspoon to the gilding water, stirring well until mixed. Then add a teaspoon of rabbit-skin size to the gilding water.

Drop some leaves of gold onto the gilder's pad and blow out a sheet so that it lies flat. Cut the leaf into 3 parts and pick up a piece with the gilder's tip. To facilitate picking up loose leaf, apply a small amount of petroleum jelly to your forearm. Brush the tip lightly over the jelly before picking up the loose leaf. Using a medium soft synthetic brush, brush the gilding water onto the area to be gilded, then apply the gold leaf to the frame.

▶ **4** Once you have applied about 6 pieces of gold leaf (2 sheets), pat down the gold with rolled-up pieces of cotton wool (cotton balls) to get rid of any air bubbles. Make sure the cotton is not wet from the patting down or it may remove the freshly applied gold.

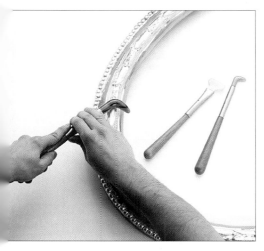

▲ **5** Once you have finished gilding the whole frame, wait for the gold to dry, about 1 hour (depending on weather conditions), then burnish with an agate burnisher passing it over the gold a number of times until the gold starts to shine. Do not press too hard as this will only weaken the gesso below.

    If you want to make the gold look older, distress it by passing over it a few times with steel wool. Make sure you do not do this in even strokes because it looks false. To prevent this from happening rub the steel wool in circular motions as well as vertically.

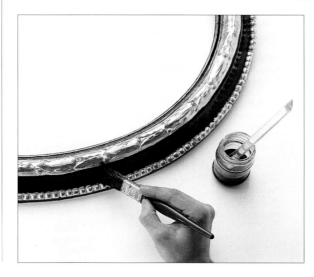

◀ **6** With a large soft synthetic brush apply a base coat of black eggshell paint. Leave to dry overnight. Apply a second coat of eggshell, making sure no dribbles occur and that any smudges that may have gone into the gold are wiped off with a rag.

▼ **7** Mix 30 ml (1 fl oz) gloss varnish with 30 ml (1 fl oz) white (mineral) spirit in a container. Use a small bristle brush to mix 1.5 cm ($\frac{1}{2}$ in) burnt umber oil colour into the varnish. Brush onto the black eggshell using one bristle brush to brush on and another dry one to brush out. Use a dry rag to wipe off any varnish which may be on the gold. Leave to dry overnight. Wax the whole of the frame using a small bristle brush to apply the wax and a soft clean rag to buff it up. Mount a mirror in the frame and then hang it in your chosen position.

Decorated Cupboard

By Dave and Kaye Ball

Painting furniture generally involves the whole piece being covered with some form of painted decoration. What is often not recognized is that the distinctions in the grain of the wood can be rich decorative elements in their own right. This cupboard is a wonderful example of how a piece of furniture can be treated to bring out the natural beauty of the wood, using painted decoration purely to enhance the inherent richness of the piece. This is the perfect piece for beginners to try, without taking the plunge of covering an entire piece of furniture with paint.

Materials and equipment

Cupboard

Stripped pine stain

500 ml (16 fl oz) acrylic paint: midnight blue

60 ml (2 fl oz) acrylic paints: grass green, vermilion, burnt gold and grey

2 soft cloths

Paintbrushes: 2.5 cm (1 in) household, Nos 4, 5 and 6 flat-ended

Carbon paper

Ballpoint pen

Crepe masking tape

Mellow wax

Preparation and tips

● Prepare the cupboard for painting according to the instructions on page 15.
● When the wood is cleaned and prepared, stain the entire cupboard both inside and out using a soft cloth to apply the stain. Apply the stain, using even strokes. Be careful not to allow too much time between applications or a great deal of overlap onto areas that have already been stained, as you will end up with dark, uneven lines and patches in the finish. If you plan to take a break, finish the section that you are working on before you stop.

▼ **1** Paint the top and bottom architraves in dark blue acrylic paint. A midnight blue was used here.

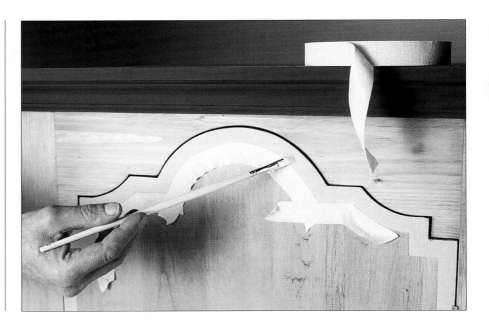

▲ **2** Lay masking tape so that you leave a 2.5 cm (1 in) border around the entire cupboard door. Crepe masking tape is suggested for use around curves. You may wish to measure your border first, making small pencil marks at intervals to line up your tape. Using a No. 6 flat-ended brush, paint in your border. Grey was used in this project. Do not remove the tape until the border has dried completely.

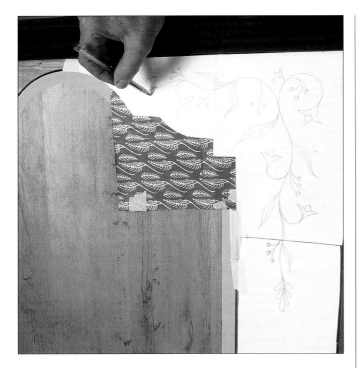

▲ **3** When the top architrave and door borders are thoroughly dry, transfer your design onto the cupboard using carbon paper (see page 12 for carbon transferring instructions). For this project, it is helpful to cut the paper that you are transferring your design from to the same shape as the cupboard door. This will help to make sure that the design is perfectly positioned.

▲ **4** Paint in your design using the acrylic paints and a No. 5 brush for filling in and a No. 4 brush for finer details. A wax finish over stained wood gives it a very rich, satin sheen. A mellow wax is suggested for this project, but see page 11 for waxing suggestions.

Chapter **2**

Kitchens and Bathrooms

Furniture, ceramics and fabrics are all crying out to be decorated in kitchens and bathrooms. In this section many different designs are given on all sorts of surfaces, but don't limit yourself to the ideas given here – free your imagination. For example, coordinating designs can be great fun. You could, say, stencil the same lemon design give on page 66 onto chairs as well as the table, and perhaps repeat it on the curtains, plates and mugs, too.

Striped and Spotted Mugs

By Lesley Harle

A set of brightly-painted mugs will brighten up any kitchen. Two very simple designs are described below, which should give you the basic skills to decorate as many mugs as you want, each with an individual pattern. You can buy mugs in a vast range of shapes and colours, offering even greater permutations.

Materials and equipment

Mugs

String

Ruler

Masking tape

Black marker pen

Self-adhesive dots

Ceramic paints: various colours

Scalpel (x-acto knife)

Paintbrushes

Carbon paper

Tracing paper

Preparation and tips

● Cold ceramic paints are meant for decorative and not utilitarian purposes. If you do want to use the mugs to drink from, it is important that you do not paint within the top 4 cm (1¹/₂ in) of the lips of the mugs, unless you intend to fire them. It is a good idea to use water-based ceramic paints that are suitable for baking in the oven (see page 8). If you mix colours to make up new shades, you must not mix water-based ceramic paints with solvent-based ones, unless the mugs are then fired.

● Mugs offer a simple opportunity for experimentation. Floral patterns, graphic approaches, and animal devices work separately or combine equally well in any number of colours, and the above examples show only a few of the thousands of possible ideas you will be able to develop.

Striped mug

▼ **1** Stick one end of a piece of string close to the rim of the mug, wrap the string around the circumference and mark the exact point at which the ends join. Remove the string from the mug, lay it down on the steel ruler – if the string will not lie flat and taut, then stick down both ends with masking tape – and measure the circumference of the mug. Decide on a convenient width for the stripes, making sure that you will have an even number of them (otherwise, you will end up with a double-width white or coloured stripe); the mug shown here has equal-width stripes. When you have calculated the spacing, you should then mark off the intervals on the piece of string using a fine black marker pen.

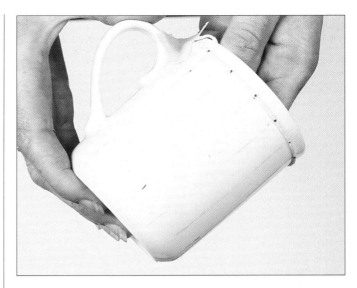

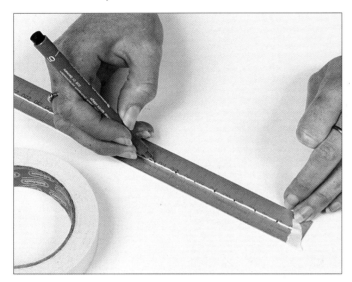

▲ **2** Stick the piece of string back first onto the top rim and then onto the bottom edge of the mug and transfer the marks from the string to the mug. Obviously, the marks need to be aligned, so use the handle of the mug as a starting point: for a neat appearance, you will want a stripe to occur centrally down the handle. This will then give you a starting point from which to mark off the rest of the stripes. When you have transferred all the marks to the mug, both top and bottom, use a ruler to draw vertical lines between them.

◄ **3** Finally, paint alternate stripes in your chosen colour. The mug shown here is painted freehand, and the vertical lines are not entirely straight. If you want more accurate lines, then you could use thin strips of masking tape along the pencil lines to cover up the white areas of the mug. Whichever method you use, the only difficulty you are likely to encounter is painting the handle – do this last, and wait about four hours for the other painted stripes to dry (do not bake them in the oven yet), so that you will be able to hold the mug firmly without the risk of smudging the paint.

Spotted mug

▶ **1** Self-adhesive dots are widely available from office stationers in a range of sizes. Initially, you will no doubt find large dots easier to deal with than smaller ones. Stick the dots down firmly all over the mug, spacing them at fairly regular intervals to give a balanced look. Cut some of the dots more or less in half to stick along the bottom edge (and to the rim of the mug if it is going to be used purely for decoration or fired). You can omit dots from the handle and leave it entirely plain as shown here – these are the trickiest to paint, especially if some of them wrap around the edge of the handle onto the underside.

▼ **2** Mix the blue ceramic paint to quite a thick consistency and paint around the self-adhesive dots. Try not to cover the dots completely with the paint, as it will be easier to remove them cleanly if you just use them as a guide. When you have painted around all the circles, allow the paint to dry to a tacky consistency. At this stage, remove the self-adhesive dots using the blade of a scalpel (x-acto knife) to ease up the edge of each one, and then pull cleanly away. Leave the paint to dry thoroughly before moving on to the next step.

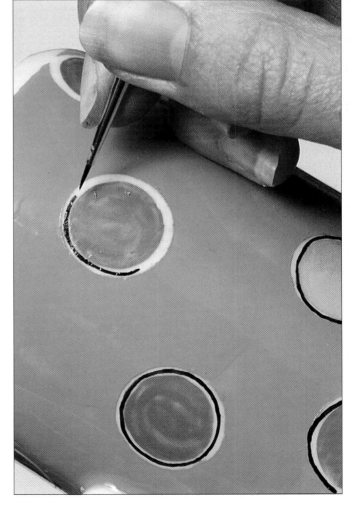

▶ **3** Mix several colours ready to paint in the spots when the blue outlines are dry. You may, of course, want to paint all the dots the same colour, but here four colours are used: pink, orange, yellow and green. Paint the spots using one colour at a time. Use the outlines left by the self-adhesive dots as a guide, but leave a thin white line between the central colour and the blue outline. Make sure that you have an even distribution of colours around the mug, so that you do not end up with, say, three or four yellow dots next to each other. Depending on your patience and dexterity, wait for each colour to dry before painting dots of a different shade, to minimize smudging.

When all the paint is thoroughly dry, paint in the outlines. Use a very fine paintbrush dipped into neat black paint.

Chunky Vegetable Dish

By Lesley Harle

Piping hot vegetables will look even more mouth-watering served from this beautiful dish, which is painted to reflect its contents — if you do not like carrots or mushrooms, you could easily substitute them with onions, turnips, tomatoes, peas or beans. Even if the dish you paint is oven-proof, cold ceramic paints are not, so make sure you cook the vegetables in a different dish and then simply transfer them to this dish, ready for serving. Do not apply decoration to the inside of the dish unless you intend to fire it, since, although non-toxic, cold ceramic paints must not come into contact with food or drink.

Materials and equipment

Vegetable dish

Black marker pen

Scalpel (x-acto knife)

Paintbrushes

Ceramic paints (water-based)

Preparation and tips

● Decide on the vegetable shapes you want to use to decorate the dish — in this case, carrots and mushrooms — and draw them onto the dish with a marking pen. The shapes here are quite crude and exaggerated, so your drawing skills do not have to be great. Given this, the design will look more effective if the vegetables are drawn quite large and bold.

● To vary the feel of the piece, paint a strong background with graphic etched devices. This will give a modern feel to the ceramic, resonant of rich winter stews.

● Alternatively, use a sponged flat colour against a plain background to produce a lighter, more spring-like feel.

▶ **1** Paint the mushrooms yellow, the carrot bodies orange and the carrot heads green. The shapes are all quite large and easy to paint, so it should not be necessary to wait for one paint to dry before applying another. If you decide to err on the side of caution and paint each colour individually, remember that the engraving must be applied before the paint is thoroughly dry.

▼ **2** Leave the paint to dry for about an hour, then start the engraving. You will need a sharp implement for this - ideally a scalpel (x-acto knife), but a small pair of scissors will suffice. Scratch away just inside the outlines of the mushrooms and carrots to suggest their gnarled surface and to give them depth. Scratching away at the paint will give different results according to how much pressure you exert on the scalpel (x-acto knife). In some instances you will lighten the colour of the paint and reveal the original white ground in others. Try to get a combination for maximum effect.

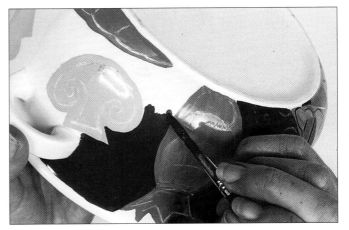

▲ **3** Wait for the paint to dry, then paint the terracotta background in. Leave the handles plain (white) and use the top lip of the dish as the upper limit of the background colour, but otherwise cover all of the body of the dish. It is not important if you do not succeed in accurately outlining the mushroom and carrot shapes – it will look like additional engraving. Again, allow the paint to dry for about an hour, then use the scalpel (x-acto knife) to scratch away small spiral shapes on the background colour. Just as there is no reason why you should paint mushrooms and carrots as opposed to beans and tomatoes, so you could just as easily engrave scrolls or diamonds in spirals.

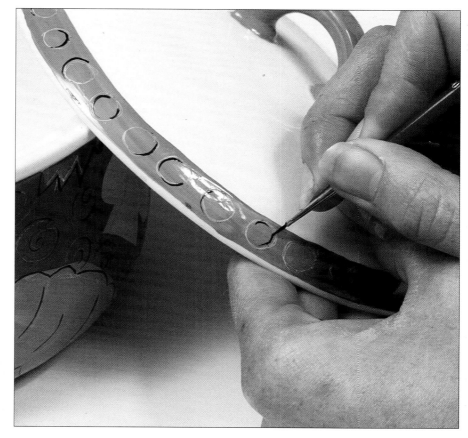

▲ **4** Outlining your work with a thin line of black paint will give it depth and definition. Wait for the terracotta colour to dry, then paint in the outlines. Use the vegetable shapes as very rough guidelines, but the outlines should be very loosely painted. Use the black paint to highlight details of the engraving, too, perhaps sweeping your brush around parts of some of the spirals and the gnarls on the carrots. Allow the black paint to dry, and the main dish is finished.

▶ **5** The lid of the dish is relatively plain. Paint the handle in the same colour as the background of the main part of the dish, and use the green paint from the carrot heads to paint a border around the edge of the lid. This can be painted freehand, using the rim of the lid as a guideline. Allow the green paint to dry for about an hour, and then scratch away roughly circular shapes in imitation of peas. When the paint is thoroughly dry, outline parts of the pea shapes in black.

Oak-patterned Chair

By Dave and Kaye Ball

With a coat of paint and a very simple decoration, this chair is given a new identity. This is a perfect example of how the simplest treatments can render dramatic results. The unusual shape of the chair back is emphasized by the curved spray of oak leaves and acorns. You could repeat the stencil design on the crossbars, if desired. This is a good piece for a beginner to try, especially if you choose a ready-made stencil instead of designing and making your own.

Materials and equipment

Wooden chair

1 litre (32 fl oz) undercoat: white

1 litre (32 fl oz) eggshell emulsion: cream

37 ml (1¼ fl oz) oil paints: viridian, yellow ochre

Paintbrushes: 2.5 cm (1 in) household; stencil

Carbon paper

Stencil paper

Ballpoint pen

Pencil

Craft knife

Masking tape

Matt varnish

Mellow wax

Preparation and tips

● Prepare the chair for painting according to the instructions on page 15. When the wood is cleaned and prepared, coat with one layer of white undercoat.
● When the undercoat has dried thoroughly, lightly sand the entire chair with fine sandpaper, dust off, and apply one even coat of base colour. Cream eggshell emulsion was used here.

▶ **1** To make the stencil, take the sketch or copy of your proposed design, and using carbon paper, transfer it to the stencil paper. Acetate can also be used. (For instructions to make acetate stencils see page 38, step 3.) The design is then cut out of the cardboard using a scalpel (x-acto knife) or craft knife.

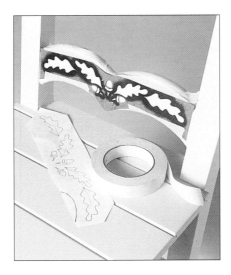

▲ **2** Position the stencil onto the chair back and secure with masking tape.

▶ **3** Place small amounts of oil paint onto a plate. Touch the tip of the stippling brush to the colour and then dab the brush tip onto a kitchen towel (paper towel) to remove excess paint before applying to the stencil. Colour should be applied in a dabbing motion rather than brushed on. You should wait at least 24 hours before varnishing or waxing (see page 11).

Alphabet Storage Jar

By Lesley Harle

Lettering can be used to personalize a variety of mass-produced ceramic objects, from initials on mugs to house names painted on plain tiles. The lettering shown here to decorate the storage jar for pasta is composed of entirely straight lines, making painting considerably simpler.

Materials and equipment

Storage jar

Tracing paper

Masking paper

Pencil

Steel ruler

Scalpel (x-acto knife)

Paintbrushes

Ceramic (or enamel) paints

Turpentine

Preparation and tips

● The alphabet shown here will enable you to paint whatever words you wish. Each letter is decorated with a different pattern.

● If you plan to letter a group of objects – whether they are storage jars, cereal bowls or mugs – you may have to alter the size of the letters according to the length of the longest word. For example, if you wanted to paint jars to hold tea, coffee and sugar, you might have to calculate the maximum size you can paint the letters in order to fit the word 'COFFEE' on one side of the jar.

● Start by tracing off the letters necessary to spell the word that you want to paint. Draw a straight line onto a piece of tracing paper and use this as a base line on which to trace the relevant letters. Use a steel ruler as you trace the letters in order to reproduce them as accurately as possible.

ABCDEFGHI
JKLMNOPQR
STUVWXYZ

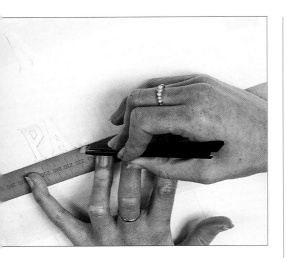

▲ **1** Cut a piece of masking paper to a size that comfortably covers the area taken up by the lettering you have traced. Place the masking paper over the tracing paper on a hard, flat cutting surface, using masking tape to stick it down firmly.

Start cutting out the letters using a steel ruler and a sharp scalpel (x-acto knife). On certain letters ('P' and 'A' in this example), you will also need to cut small pieces of masking paper that mask out the middle.

Measure the height of the storage line from the base to the top rim of the main part of the jar. Measure a point about half way up the jar as a base line for the lettering to sit on and mark this in three places. Join up the points to form a horizontal line. Measure the width of the front face of the jar and mark the mid point in three places; join up these points to form a vertical line. These lines will enable you to position the lettering accurately. Carefully peel away the masking paper from the tracing paper and stick onto the storage jar using the pencil guidelines you have just drawn: the bottom edge of the lettering should sit exactly on the horizontal line and the middle letter (in this example, the 'S') should be centred on the vertical line. Firmly rub along the edges of the lettering with your finger nail to make sure that the masking paper is securely stuck down. Remember to stick in the pieces of masking paper to mask out the centres of certain letters, such as 'A', 'B', 'O' etc.

▲ **2** Start painting the letters in black, or whatever colour you have decided on. Apply the paint with some caution so that you minimize the risk of the paint seeping underneath the masking paper. Allow the paint to dry until it is sticky (about 20 minutes) and then gently peel away the masking paper. Use a fine paintbrush and turpentine to remove unwanted blemishes. Leave the paint to dry thoroughly.

▲ **3** When the lettering is completely dry you can apply the white decorative patterns. Use a fine paintbrush and undiluted white ceramic paint or enamel paint. Each letter in the alphabet illustrated is decorated with a different pattern, and some of the designs require more skill than others to apply. You may, of course, want to leave the lettering entirely plain; alternatively, you could apply just one design to all of the letters, or just to recurring ones.

Lemon-painted Table

By Jane Brossard and Sandra Krivine

Small wooden tables are very easy to come by, as well as inexpensive. Instead of draping them with a circular tablecloth, use paint to give an individual look. This table has been transformed from a forgotten relic into a lovely addition to any garden or sun room. Colourful fruit stencils were used for the designs on the border and legs, and the weathered or 'distressed' look is easily achieved with a fine-grade sandpaper and a delicate hand. The legs were entwined with ribbon stencils and contrasting coloured bows were added to the crossbars as a finishing touch. You can keep to conventional colours for the fruit or choose your own colour scheme.

Preparation and tips

● Prepare the table for painting according to the instructions on page 15. When the wood is cleaned and prepared, apply one coat of white undercoat and allow to dry.
● When the white basecoat has dried thoroughly, sand the entire piece lightly with fine-grade sandpaper or wire wool to create a smooth finish, but taking care not to remove patches of paint. Apply a second coat of emulsion, but using soft blue instead of white, and leave to dry.
● To make a soft blue, gradually add white emulsion, and water if necessary, to the blue emulsion paint until you achieve a satisfactory pale blue colour.
● Finally, paint on a third coat of emulsion using mostly white (with a touch of the soft blue from the previous coat), and grey, mixed to your personal taste.

Materials and equipment

Wooden table

1 litre (32 fl oz) undercoat: white

1 litre (32 fl oz) emulsion: blue

Grey emulsion

60 ml (2 fl oz) acrylic paints: lemon yellow, yellow ochre, lime green, forest green, purple, crimson

Paintbrushes: 2.5 cm (1 in) household; stencil

Glass jam jar

Masking tape

Clear acetate or oiled paper

Permanent ink pen

Scalpel (x-acto knife)

2 soft cloths

Matt varnish

Wax polish

Sandpaper (fine)

▶ **1** While the emulsion coat is still slightly wet, gently wipe with a cloth until you begin to see the soft blue from the second undercoat showing through. This same effect can also be achieved by waiting for the paint to dry and lightly sanding with a piece of fine-grade sandpaper.

▼ **2** The stencils are made by tracing your chosen design onto a piece of acetate with a permanent ink pen, and then cutting the form out with a scalpel (x-acto knife). A more detailed description of this technique can be found on page 38, steps 3 and 4. Before you begin to paint, use the stencil and measure your basic design onto the surface by marking each end of the stencil (in this case the lemon) lightly with a pencil. When you are ready to paint, line the stencil up with a set of your pencil marks, and tape it to the surface to keep it from moving while you paint. Use a brush to dab the paint over the stencil. (Hints on stippling technique can be found on page 15.)

▲ **3** When the lemons have dried, use yellow ochre around the edges to give them more depth and dimension. Reposition the stencil if it has already been removed, and lightly stipple at the edges with the darker colour.

▲ **4** For the leaves, the same technique is used as for the lemons, beginning with a lighter colour (lime green), and shading with a darker forest green.

When the leaves have dried, stencil in the other small fruit and flowers.

▲ **5** To achieve an aged or 'distressed' look, lightly sand over the painted surface with a fine piece of sandpaper.

◄ **6** As the legs of the table are very plain, a stencil cut to look like ribbon was used down the legs. A heavier stippling technique was used at the ends of the stencil (this means using more pressure as opposed to more paint on the brush), leaving the centres light. This creates a satin effect as well as giving the impression that the ribbon is wrapped around the legs of the table.

The stencilled purple bows on the crossbars are an attractive finishing touch. When all the paint is entirely dry, paint two coats of matt varnish. If you prefer a richer matt finish then add two coats of wax polish.

Strawberry Bowl

By Lesley Harle

This colourful fruit bowl is easier to paint than you might imagine. Although the design illustrated uses strawberries, you could just as easily choose apples, oranges, lemons, pears, bananas or any other fruit. The bowl shown here is quite large, although you could apply the fruit motifs to smaller bowls. However, in that case, it would be wise to scale down the size of the strawberries to maintain a good sense of proportion.

Materials and equipment

Bowl

String

Pencil

Tracing paper

Carbon paper

Ruler

Tape measure

Masking tape

Paintbrushes

Cold ceramic paint

Masking fluid (optional)

Preparation and tips

● Cold ceramic paints are not food-safe: unless you choose to take the additional precautions necessary to make your bowl food-safe, paint only on the outside of the bowl, finishing under its lip so that you can be certain that no fruit could come into contact with the painted area.

● Measure around the top rim of the bowl using a piece of string to discover the circumference (see Striped Mug, page 54, step 1). Draw a line to the length of the circumference of the bowl onto a piece of tracing paper, and then draw a second line parallel to the first – this represents the depth of the border at the top of the rim. In this design, the border represents about one-seventh of the total depth of the bowl, so you can calculate what the measurement should be for your own bowl. Having drawn out flat the area representing the bowl, draw a scroll shape on a separate piece of paper to a size that will fit comfortably within the space available. Measure the length of the scroll and calculate how many scrolls you will need for the border, taking into consideration an equal spacing of 3–6 mm ($^1/_8$ – $^1/_4$in) between each scroll.

● Use a tape measure to mark the depth of the border at various points on the rim of the bowl, then join up the points with as straight a line as possible. Next mark on the rim of the bowl the starting and finishing points of each scroll. Trace the scroll shape onto a piece of tracing paper, and, using carbon paper, transfer the scroll motif to the bowl (see Techniques, page 12), using the marks on the rim of the bowl and the line you have drawn in to make sure they are correctly positioned. Work your way around the rim of the bowl until all the scrolls are traced in position.

▶ **1** With the border design transferred, use a damp cloth to wipe away the spacing marks and paint in the lime green background, leaving the scroll shapes white (blank) for the time being. If you are nervous about painting around the scrolls accurately, you can mask them out using watercolour masking fluid (see Basic Techniques, page 14).

▼ **2** Draw or trace off and enlarge a strawberry shape from the photograph and transfer it onto the bowl. This design includes two strawberry shapes, and by using both you can add slightly more variation to your bowl. However, the most important thing is to transfer the strawberry design at approximately regular intervals and rotate the strawberries so that some are on their sides, some upside down, etc. Use portions of the strawberry shape at the edge of the border and at the base.

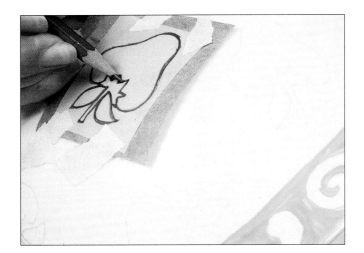

▲ **3** Mix a red of the appropriate shade and paint in the strawberry. Cover the whole area taken up by the body of the fruit – the small white dots are painted on later. Allow the red paint to dry thoroughly.

Next, paint in the lime green stalks of the strawberries. When these, too, are dry, paint the dark green around the base of the bowl (if applicable), the leaves and the scrolls (remember to remove the masking fluid first if you used that method – see Basic Techniques, page 14). Use the dark green to paint the base first, then go back and paint the leaves and scrolls, rotating the bowl until they are all done. (If you leave the base until last, you may smudge the newly-painted scrolls as you try to turn the bowl around.)

◀ **4** Wait for the dark green paint to dry. Using a fine paintbrush dipped in pure white paint, apply small dots to the bodies of the strawberries. Finally, use a very fine paintbrush and neat black paint to outline the strawberries and the scroll shapes, and to paint in the central vein of each leaf. The design thrives on the vibrant, hand-painted look, so you do not have to apply the outlines with perfect accuracy.

Abstract Roller Blind

By Delaine le Bas

Painted roller blinds were very much in vogue from the seventeenth century onwards, providing a charming and peaceful focal point. Today, blinds often replace curtains, and they need not be dull, as this swirling cylinder-printed example demonstrates. Tin cans are opened at both ends, cleaned, and then filled with small amounts of pigment in a variety of colours. When these 'cylinders' are pulled across the fabric from side to side, the paint swirls together and is deposited on the fabric in a marbled effect. Four colours were used in varying combinations for this blind — pick out colours from existing furnishings and combine them to make a complementary blind.

Materials and equipment

Bleached cotton

Newspapers

Double-sided tape

Tin cans

Fabric paints

Iron

Preparation and tips

● For the best effect, choose tin cans in a variety of sizes, and thoroughly wash them before using.
● Wash the bleached cotton to remove manufacturer's finish.
● Place the washed and ironed cotton on a flat worksurface covered with several thicknesses of newspaper.
● Secure the fabric to the surface with lengths of double-sided tape.

▶ **1** Remove the bottom as well as the top of the tin can to leave a metal cylinder. Be careful not to leave any sharp edges. Make sure that the can is scrupulously clean and free from grease before you begin. Carefully place small amounts of three or four colours of fabric paint on the newspaper visible at the bottom of the can.

▶ **2** Immediately pull the can across the fabric. The different coloured paints will mix inside the can as it slides across the fabric to produce a swirling marbled effect. When you reach the other side of the blind, continue onto the newspaper so that the excess paint can be deposited there without staining the blind.

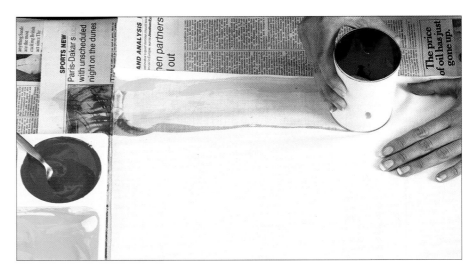

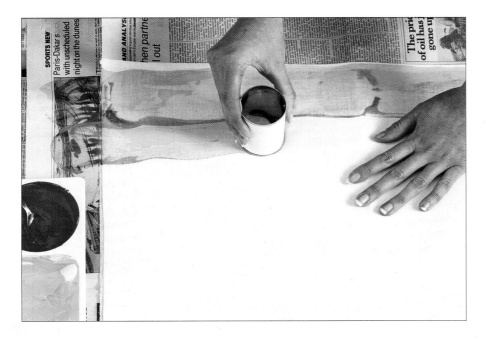

◀ **3** Repeat this process to produce the second band of marbling, using the same (cleaned) can, or another smaller or larger one to give a variegated effect. The wider the mouth of the can, the thicker the band of colour will be.

Repeat the cylinder printing until the fabric is covered, and then allow it to dry thoroughly. Iron the blind on the reverse through a sheet of paper and following the paint manufacturer's instructions. When the paint is permanently fixed, attach the blind to wooden rollers from a roller blind kit.

Decorative Kitchen Cupboard

By Dave and Kaye Ball

Every kitchen can use an extra storage space for the spices and jars that seem to accumulate on the counters and table. By using an unpainted cupboard, you can create a design that fits your decor as if it had always been part of the kitchen; or choose a bright pattern to add some vibrancy, and make your cupboard a focal point of the room.

Look for inspiration for your design in tea towels, oven gloves, and plate patterns; and for colour suggestions, try wall tiles, plates, and curtains.

Materials and equipment

Kitchen cupboard

Stripped pine stain

500 ml (16 fl oz) undercoat: white

500 ml (16 fl oz) emulsion paint: lemon yellow

60 ml (2 fl oz) acrylic paints: light blue, dark green, vermilion, black, white

2 soft cloths

Paintbrushes: 2.5 cm (1 in) household; No. 8 filbert; Nos 4 and 6 detail

Carbon paper

Masking tape

Ballpoint pen

Matt varnish or mellow wax

Preparation and tips

● Prepare the cabinet for painting according to the instructions on page 15. As you will be applying a stain, be sure to fill any holes with a neutral wood filler; other types may darken when the stain is applied. When the wood is cleaned and prepared, apply the stain evenly using a soft cloth.

● To avoid dark, uneven lines and patches in the finish, be careful not to leave too much time between applications or allow a great deal of overlap onto areas that have already been stained.

● If you plan to take a break, finish the section that you are working on before stopping.

● To make the light yellow paint, thoroughly mix the lemon yellow emulsion with some white until you have achieved the desired colour.

▲ **1** Using the 2.5 cm (1 in) household brush, apply white undercoat to the inner door panels. Carefully clean the 2.5 cm (1 in) brush, and, working in stages, use it to paint the rest of the cupboard with light yellow emulsion or with the colour of your choice.

▶ **2** As you paint, use a soft cloth to gently wipe over the wet areas to allow the stain to show through slightly. Be sure to work in small sections, as the larger the area you are painting, the greater the chance that the paint will dry slightly before you have a chance to wipe over it.

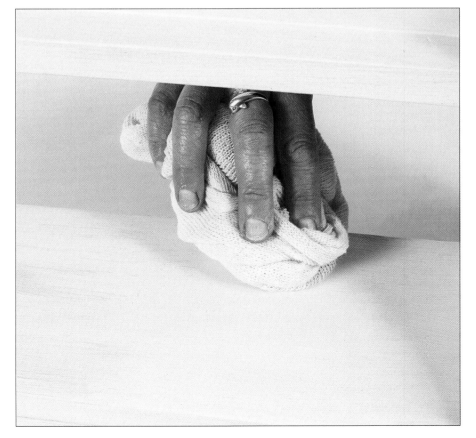

▼ **3** Using a No. 8 filbert brush, paint the beading around the edges of the door panel. A light blue was used here.

▲ **4** The design for the front panel is easily transferred by taping down a piece of carbon paper to the door, taping your design over it and tracing with a ballpoint pen. Try not to press down too hard, as you will make an impression in the wood. Also, try not to rub against the carbon while you are transferring your design, as it will leave smudge marks. The decoration is painted in using Nos 4 and 6 detail brushes and warm, simple colours. After the base colours have dried slightly, add darker touches to the edges of the berries and the centres of the leaves to create the effect of depth and dimension.

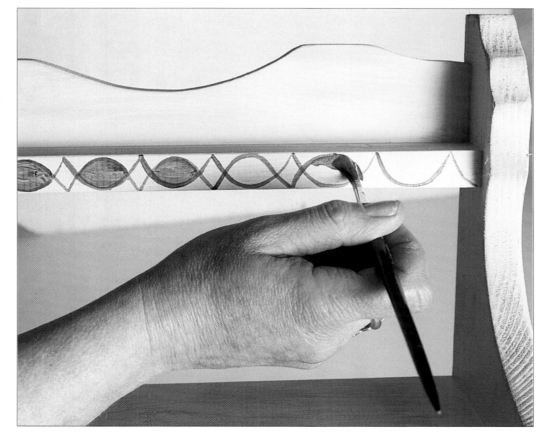

◄ **5** The top border design, consisting of overlapping arches, can either be painted free-hand or sketched in with a pencil before you begin painting. Finish with either a matt varnish or a mellow wax.

Blue Stencilled Tiles

By Lesley Harle

Stencilling is one of the quickest and simplest ways to decorate ceramics, and flat tiles are the easiest surface on which to apply the technique. The design shown here is very basic, and is a good project to start on if you are not confident of your skills. You could add extra interest by stencilling tiles in alternate colours or by adding a border.

Materials and equipment

Pencil

Tracing paper

Stencil paper or thin cardboard

Sponge or tissues

Masking tape

Cold ceramic paint: blue

Paintbrush: fine

Preparation and tips

● Trace the motif from the photograph opposite and enlarge as necessary to fit your tile size. Transfer it centrally onto a piece of stencil paper or thin cardboard measuring the same dimensions as the tiles. If you want to stencil enough tiles to cover a wall, then it is best to use stencil paper, since this will not become soggy with repeated use. If your tiles are of different dimensions, then you will have to enlarge or reduce the design to fit (see Basic Techniques, page 12).

● On each of the tiles that you want to stencil, mark the middle of each side and then draw a line with a pencil from the top to the bottom and from the left-hand to the right-hand side. Use these four lines as guides for centralizing the motif on the tile: the four points of the motif should align with the pencil lines drawn on the tile. With the motif centred as accurately as possible, stick the stencil to the tile using masking tape. Wipe off the pencil marks from the area to be stencilled, using a damp cloth.

▲ **1** Paint the central motif using a sponge or tissue dipped into cold ceramic paint. Use a scrap of paper to remove excess paint from the sponge and begin filling in the motif. If you want the motif to appear quite bold, you will probably have to repeat the process a second or even a third time. For a more textured effect, use a second colour, but experiment on a scrap of paper first to make sure the two colours harmonize.

▲ **2** Work the paint into the edges of the stencil using a small piece of sponge or tissue, holding the stencil paper down with your spare hand to prevent paint seeping onto the masked-out area of the tile. Take up a small amount of paint onto a fine paintbrush and very gently draw it around the outline of the stencil, being careful not to draw too obvious a line.

▲ **3** Remove the stencil from the tile, and, again using a fine paintbrush, lightly dab along the edge of the motif so that it is clearly defined, but be careful to retain the sponged look. Wait for the paint to dry thoroughly, and then wipe away all the pencil lines that had formed the 'grid'.

▲ **4** To create a tessellated look, wait for the paint on the centred stencil motif to dry thoroughly, wipe away the pencil line. Then use the edges of the tiles to line up the relevant quarter of the stencil, just as you did with the pencil lines. Stick the stencil in place and apply it exactly as before. You can also create an attractive border along the top row of tiles by stencilling just half of the motif against one edge.

Folk Art Bathroom Cabinet

By Dave and Kaye Ball

Painting a simple wooden bathroom cabinet is an excellent way to brighten up a bathroom while creating extra storage space for the inevitable accumulation of creams, brushes and tubes. The colours in this piece are slightly subdued, but you can easily adapt them to suit your own colour scheme. Try looking at towels and tiles, or window and shower curtains for inspiration for your paints.

The pattern on the doors is transferred using carbon paper, and painting it is just a matter of staying within the lines. For inspiration for the patterns, try books on folk art, or special pattern books. Fabric is also a useful source. Find a design that you like and photocopy it, or combine a number of patterns to create a new one.

Materials and equipment

Wooden cabinet

1 litre (32 fl oz) undercoat: white

60 ml (2 oz) acrylic paints: midnight blue, grass green, holly green, vermilion, yellow ochre

Paintbrushes: 2.5 cm (1 in) household; Nos 4 and 5 sable detail; No. 6 flat-ended sable

Carbon paper

Ballpoint pen

Masking tape

Matt varnish

Mellow wax

Preparation and tips

● Prepare the cabinet for painting according to the instructions on page 15. When the wood is cleaned and prepared, coat with one layer of white undercoat, and allow to dry thoroughly.
● When the white basecoat has dried thoroughly, sand the entire piece lightly with fine-grade sandpaper or wire wool to create a smooth finish, but taking care not to remove patches of paint.

▼ **1** Using a No. 6 flat brush, paint the mirror frame, front borders, and door panel frames. Grass green was used here. Carefully clean the No. 6 brush, and use it to paint the top architrave and the front strip of the lower shelf in holly green.

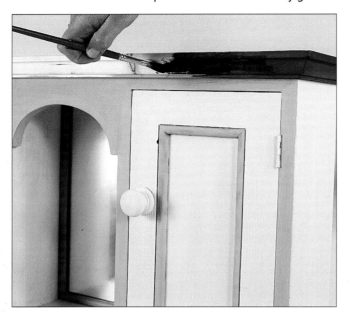

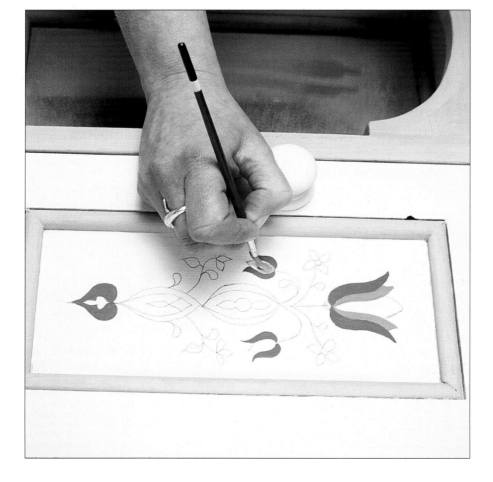

▲ **2** The design for the front panel is easily transferred by taping a piece of carbon paper to the door, taping your design over it and tracing down with a ballpoint pen. Try not to press down too hard, as you will make an impression in the wood. Also, try not to rub against the carbon while transferring the design, as it will leave smudge marks.

◄ **3** To fill in the design, a No. 5 sable brush works well and a No. 4 brush can be used for finer details and thin lines. Finish with either a matt varnish or a mellow wax as you prefer. See page 11 for suggestions.

Chapter

3

Bedrooms

There are so many surfaces in a bedroom that can be painted to add originality and flair. Start with the bedhead and bedlinen, and then move onto the furniture – a very simply colourwashed wardrobe is so straightforward.

Then there are those small finishing touches for the treasured family photographs. In this chapter there are projects for decorating a picture mount with a neat stencil, and a more ambitious piece of gilding around the picture frame itself.

Floral Bed

By Jill Hancock

An imaginatively painted bed will easily become the centrepiece of the entire bedroom. This bed in particular, with its whimsical ducks and brightly painted flowers, is sure to become a family treasure.

Although the border and many of the details are hand-painted, the techniques for creating this design are as simple as they are effective. A template is used for the more complicated flowers; and the ducks, with their wonderful relief effect, are actually attached after they are decorated.

The sheer size of the piece may make the project seem rather daunting, but the surfaces are flat and therefore excellent to work on, and the simplicity of the painting techniques employed makes it both quick and enjoyable, even though the finished product looks as if it was difficult and time-consuming.

Materials and equipment

Standard double bed

1 litre (32 fl oz) undercoat: white

500 ml (16 fl oz) vinyl matt emulsion: grass green

1 litre (32 fl oz) vinyl matt emulsion: green

60 ml (2 fl oz) acrylic paints: light green, sky blue, navy blue, yellow ochre, red, gold

Paintbrushes: 5 cm (2 in) household; range of artist's detail; stippling (optional)

4 mm (1/6 in) birchfaced plywood

Pencil

Coping saw

White glue or 12 brass panel pins

1 litre (32 fl oz) poly-gloss varnish

Sandpapers (fine- and medium-grades)

Preparation and tips

● Prepare the bed for painting according to the instructions on page 15. When the wood is cleaned and prepared, apply two coats of white undercoat, allowing the first to dry before applying the second, and making sure that all areas are covered.

● After each coat has dried, sand the entire piece lightly with fine-grade sandpaper or wire wool to create a smooth finish, taking care not to remove patches of paint.

● To make other colours in the design such as cream and orange, mix together the appropriate acrylic paints from those listed to the right.

▶ **1** Using a 5 cm (2 in) household brush, paint a thin coat of slightly watered down, grass green vinyl matt emulsion over the front panel of the bed. Before this dries (and as it is watered down it dries very quickly), use either the end of the brush you are already painting with, or a special stippling brush with stiff bristles, to meticulously dab the wet paint to create a grass-like effect.

▶ **2** When the grass area has dried, the tree-line can be created by applying forest green acrylic with a thick detail brush, using short but sweeping strokes. While the forest green is still damp, blend in light green and yellow ochre acrylic paints to highlight some of the leaves.

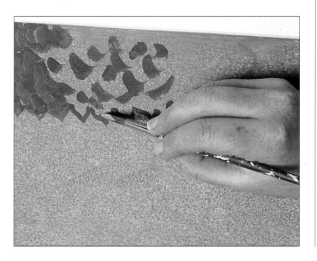

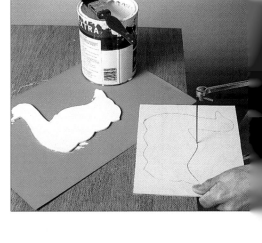

▲ **3** The iris template and the ducks are both drawn freehand onto pieces of birchfaced plywood, cut out with a coping saw, and then sanded with a medium-grade sandpaper until the edges are smooth. The iris template can be made from thin cardboard instead of wood and cut with scissors or a scalpel (x-acto knife).

If you don't feel comfortable with your freehand drawing ability, find a flower design which when folded in half is the same on both sides, and use the paper cardboard template technique described on page 13. The ducks can also be painted directly onto the bed using the wood form as a template.

◀ **4** Measure and trace the irises onto the bed, making sure you leave enough space between them to fit the ducks in. If you make a light mark on either side of the template, at each place you plan to position a flower and before making the final traces, you can do any repositioning necessary as you have not fully marked the paint.

At this point, paint any area that is going to receive painted decoration with one layer of white acrylic. This includes painting in the traced irises, the apples and the water-line. If you have decided to paint the ducks directly onto the bed, block them too. If not, the wooden cut-outs need to be coated with one layer of white. Don't forget that you can see the edges of the wood when the ducks are attached to the bed, so they should be painted too.

► **5** When the white paint is dry, paint in the water-line, the irises, and the apples in solid blocks of colour. While the apples are still damp, blend in a touch of the yellow ochre to highlight and give them fullness and depth.

To paint the daisies, first paint the yellow centres by lightly touching the tip of the brush to the surface, and then painting thin white lines out from the centres for the petals. If you want to be more exact, use a pencil to make a small mark where you want the daisies to be painted. Remember, if you are attaching the ducks at the end, you don't need to paint daisies in the spaces that the ducks will be covering.

▼ **6** The border detail simply requires painting a strip of blue, waiting for that to dry, and then painting in a row of dark green triangles and daisies over the top. Paint in the orange borders as well.

The final painting touch is to outline the leaves and detail the outer borders with gold acrylic. Notice how the use of the gold detail on the bed-posts along with some of the other colours from the decorative design gives a complete overall effect.

▲ **7** Now you can go back and decorate the ducks. Remember to allow each colour to dry thoroughly before applying another colour over it. Using slightly different colour combinations on each duck, or alternating two colour patterns will give the bed a livelier look. When the ducks have dried, attach them to the bed using either white glue or brass panel pins.

To seal and protect the paint, give the entire bed one coat of a standard poly-gloss varnish. Try to cover evenly, being careful not to let the varnish accumulate around the edges of the wooden ducks, or to leave drip marks in the finish.

Country Armoire

By Dave and Kaye Ball

This full-length cupboard is treated with a beautifully subtle finish using eggshell paint and scumble glaze. This simple treatment is excellent to use on any size of cupboard. The textured effect is easily achieved by wiping the paint with a soft cloth to reveal the basecoat. You could also apply this technique to hand-made built-in wardrobes to give them a unique hand-painted look.

Materials and equipment

Armoire

2 litres (64 fl oz) undercoat: white

500 ml (16 fl oz) eggshell paint: green

Scumble glaze

White (mineral) spirit

Paintbrushes: 5 cm (2 in) household; stippling; No. 6 flat-ended sable

Soft cloth

White (mineral) spirit

Matt varnish

Preparation and tips

● Prepare the armoire for painting according to the instructions on page 15. When the wood is cleaned and prepared, coat the entire piece with two layers of white undercoat, allowing to dry thoroughly and sanding lightly with a fine-grade sandpaper after each coat has dried.

▶ **1** Beginning with the sides, and using a 5 cm (2 in) brush, apply the following glaze mixture to the armoire: 4 tablespoons of scumble glaze, 2 tablespoons of green eggshell paint, and 4 tablespoons of white (mineral) spirit. Everything except the top and bottom architrave, and the door panels, should be coated in the glaze mixture. As you paint, use a soft cloth to gently wipe over the wet areas in order to create a washed effect.

◀ **2** Mix up a slightly darker glaze, and paint in the door panels. While the paint is still damp, use a stippling brush and a firm patting motion. Wipe the brush frequently to remove the paint that has accumulated. It is best to paint and stipple each panel at a time as stippling will only be successful on a damp surface.

▶ **3** Apply an even coating of the glaze mixture to the panel mouldings using a No. 6 detail brush and a long dragging stroke to obtain an even coating.

▼ **4** Apply the same dark glaze that was used on the panels and moulding to the top and bottom architraves.

While the paint is still wet, wipe off with a soft dry cloth using a smooth, even motion. Finish off with two coats of matt varnish.

Block-printed Bedlinen

By Suzanna Holland

The patchy, antique appearance of this beautifully embellished bedlinen is achieved using an ancient decorative technique called frottage. This entails rubbing pigment onto a surface over a textured background to create an uneven, grainy effect. Concrete floors, unplaned wood, pebbled areas and slate floors all make good textural surfaces. If none of these is available, make a 'portable' surface by covering a piece of thin wood with filler in a rough, peaked texture.

Materials and equipment

Pure cotton pillowcases

Iron

Thin wood

All-purpose filler

Cardboard

Fabric paints: various colours

Pencil

Preparation and tips

● Cut the thin wood to size to fit the pillowcases. Mix up a bowl of filler and roughly cover the board to make a textured surface, spreading the filler with a small piece of cardboard. Allow the board to dry thoroughly.

● Wash, dry and press the pillowcases.

● Cover your worksurface with heavy plastic. Insert the textured board into the middle of one of the pillowcases. This will prevent paint bleeding through and staining the second layer of cotton, as well as providing a patterned surface for the design.

▶ **1** Apply the border colour to the cotton using a small piece of cardboard. So that the texture of the board comes through press down quite hard onto the pillowcase.

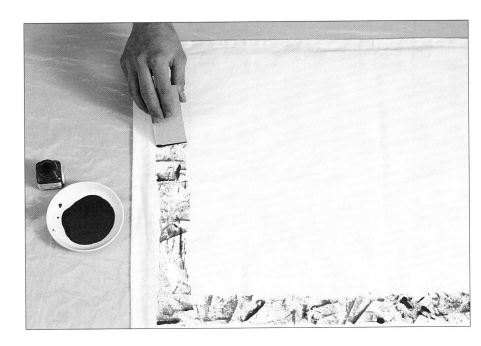

▼ **2** Using a smaller piece of thick card, decorate the centre of the pillowcase in the same way with a contrasting colour. The smaller the piece of card, the narrower the width of the textured design produced. Continue to build up the design using a variety of different shades and strokes.

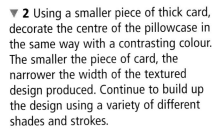

▲ **3** Add smaller details using the blunt end of a pencil dipped in paint. Again, if you press hard, the texture of the board will show on the pillowcase.

◀ **4** When the fabric paint has dried thoroughly, remove the cardboard from the inside of the pillowcase and iron through a length of thin cotton to fix the paint following the manufacturer's instructions. Experiment with matching trims or whole sheets to make a coordinating set of bedlinen.

American Indian Chest of Drawers

By Dave and Kayè Ball

This chest of drawers employs the carbon transfer technique (see page 12) for creating the American Indian design on the drawer fronts, and is a particularly good illustration of how ideas for painting furniture can be culturally inspired.

The pattern has been adapted to fit the two smaller drawer fronts and even the knobs have been cleverly incorporated into the overall design. The strong blue lines on top and base bring the design together well.

Materials and equipment

Chest of drawers

1 litre (32 fl oz) undercoat: white

1 litre (32 fl oz) acrylic paint: turquoise

60 ml (2 fl oz) acrylic paints: midnight blue, grass green, rust, yellow ochre

Paintbrushes: 4 cm (1 1/2 in) household; Nos 5 and 6 artist's

Soft cloth

Carbon paper

Masking tape

Ballpoint pen

Wax or varnish

Sandpaper (fine-grade)

Preparation and tips

● Prepare the chest for painting according to the instructions on page 15.
● When the wood is cleaned and prepared, remove all the drawers and then all the handles from the drawers. Apply one coat of white undercoat, being careful not to forget the edges of the drawer fronts, inside drawer frames, edges of legs, and the under edge of the top. After allowing to dry, lightly sand the entire piece with a fine-grade sandpaper, taking care not to remove patches of paint.

▼ **1** Working in stages, apply turquoise paint to the sides and front first and then the top.

After each stage, allow the paint to set, although not to dry. Using a damp cloth, wipe the paint off working in the direction of the grain of the wood.

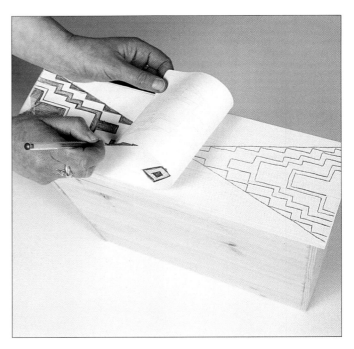

▲ **2** While the turquoise is drying, transfer your design to the drawer fronts using carbon paper (see page 12). Make sure that when you draw your design it is the exact size of the drawer you are decorating.

◀ **3** For this design, No. 5 and No. 6 artist's detail brushes will be sufficient for painting in the decoration. For a design with finer details, you may wish to use a No. 4 brush.

▼ **4** Using midnight blue, paint the outside edge of the chest of drawers top and the top edge of the plinth.

Finish with either wax or varnish depending on the effect that you desire (see page 11 for details).

Gilded Picture Frame

By Rodrigo Titian

A simple flat frame is used here. The application of the raised gesso motif is quite an old technique and the lines blend in well with the flowing brush strokes of the painting itself. The painting has been framed professionally and complements the soft yellow varnish used on the frame. The fact that silver leaf has been used below the yellow varnish gives the impression of the frame having been water gilded in gold leaf.

Preparation and tips

● If the frame has any cracks or chips that need filling, repair them using putty or filler. Then make the gesso by adding 1 part prepared rabbit-skin size to 1 part cold water. Sieve in just enough gesso powder to colour the liquid and stir well. When applied, the gesso should appear translucent. Heat the liquid over a bain-marie until it is hot, but not boiling.

● Prepare the frame with a first coat of gesso and leave to dry for 24 hours. Then using a gesso brush, apply 4-6 coats of gesso in even, generous strokes, leaving about half the amount for the next stages. Allow 15 minutes for each coat to dry.

● Choose a fairly simple design and transfer it to tracing paper. Transfer this to your frame with a soft lead pencil, making sure it is clear and sharp.

Materials and equipment

Flat-sided picture frame

Putty or filler (optional)

Rabbit-skin size

Gesso powder

Paintbrushes: gesso; small sable; large flat hog; small bristle

Tracing paper

Soft lead pencil

Soft rags

Clays: yellow, black

Silicone carbide sandpaper

Dusting brush

Methylated spirit (wood alcohol)

Gilder's pad, knife and tip

2 books silver loose leaf

Petroleum jelly

Cotton wool (cotton balls)

Small agate burnisher

Fine steel wool

Transparent polish (shellac)

Polishing rubber

Gloss varnish

White (mineral) spirit

Oil paints: Indian yellow, crimson lake, burnt sienna

Badger brush

▶ **1** Heat the leftover gesso solution in a bain-marie until it becomes liquid. Using a small sable brush, apply the gesso to the lines of the design by dropping it on gently and gradually building it up until a raised motif is achieved. Allow to dry overnight. Rub down the gesso using a rag dipped into luke-warm water. Pass this over the frame in a circular motion until the gesso is ivory smooth. Allow to dry for 10 minutes.

▼ **2** Mix the yellow clay solution as described in step 1 on page 46 and heat it in a bain-marie. Using a large flat hog brush, apply this all over the surface of the frame as evenly as possible. Leave to dry for about 10 minutes. A second coat of yellow clay can be applied if a deeper colour is desired.

▲ **3** Mix and heat up the black clay solution as for the yellow clay solution in a bain-marie. When the mixture becomes liquid apply it to the raised motif only, using a small sable brush. Leave to dry for about 10 minutes.

Smooth down the clays using silicone carbide sandpaper until they are smooth to the touch. When you have done this, dust well with a dusting brush.

◀ **4** Mix the gilding water as described in step 3 on page 46 and add a pea-sized blob of yellow clay solution. Prepare your gilder's pad with a few sheets of silver leaf. Brush on the gilding water in small sections and, using the gilder's tip, lay on the silver cut to a rough size (see also step 3 on page 46 for advice on using the tip). After every 5 minutes of gilding, pat down the silver with cotton wool (cotton balls) to make sure there are no air bubbles. Allow between 1 and 2 hours to dry.

Using a small agate burnisher, burnish only the raised area.

▲ **5** Distress the silver using steel wool. Do this until you can see the clay colours just coming through. Use a dusting brush to remove any steel wool fragments. Make some fixing polish by mixing 60 per cent methylated spirit (wood alcohol) with 40 per cent transparent polish (shellac) in a jar and apply a thin coat to fix the silver using a polishing rubber.

▲ **6** Mix a varnish of 50 per cent gloss varnish to 50 per cent white (mineral) spirit and, using a small bristle brush, add 2.5 cm (1 in) of each oil colour to produce a yellow hue. Apply this to the frame using the same brush. Using a dry medium brush, spread the colour out evenly before it dries so as not to leave streaks or puddles.

◄ **7** Finally, use a badger brush to soften the colour and remove any varnish streaks, again making sure this is done before the varnish becomes touch-dry.

Stencilled Picture Mount

By Vivien Frank

It is possible to use a stencil to decorate a mount for a picture or photograph without going to a great deal of trouble. There are suitable stencils available ready-made or you can design your own. If the mount is for a specific picture or photograph, an element from the picture can be used to create the stencil; alternatively a more traditional approach, which suits general needs, can be chosen. The mount can either be purchased, or cut to fit if the picture is an unusual size.

Materials and equipment

Purchased mount, or mount board and mount cutter

Stencil material

Scrap paper

Coloured pencils

Masking tape

Preparation and tips

● Prepare the mount to the chosen size or take a purchased mount and, on a piece of scrap paper, draw around the outside and the window, being careful not to make any marks on the mount.

◄ **1** Take the prepared stencil and, on the scrap paper, draw the shapes to check that the planned design looks pleasing and well balanced. The example shown here has been carried out using coloured pencils, which give a soft appearance.

▼ **2** When the design is right, fix the stencil in place on the mount with small pieces of masking tape, which can be easily removed without marking. Work the design methodically and when the first area has been finished, lift the stencil and reposition it to complete the design.

◄ **3** If you are using paints and commercial stencils, the stencil will have to be removed and the paint allowed to dry before more colours are added so that no smudging occurs. These stencils usually have dotted lines printed on the second area to be coloured that act as registration marks.

4

Nurseries

The nursery is probably the most frequently decorated room of the house. With the imminent arrival of a baby, the paintbrushes always seem to be brought out with great alacrity. So here are five charming ideas to get you going. A cradle for the tiniest of infants is decorated in the Dutch folk style and a papier mâché mobile can be fixed above it to entertain the baby during those wakeful moments. For all animal-loving toddlers, there is a cat toy box and chicken cushion, and the whole section is rounded off with some brightly stencilled nursery curtains.

Cat Toy Box

By Jill Hancock

A child's toy box is not only a storage place for toys, but something they will play in, on and around. Any child would love the bold colours and the happy, animated cats on this painted chest, particularly when it has been created especially for them. The basic painted treatment is relatively straightforward with a few simple freehand accents. The cats, which are the focus of the box, are attached after they are decorated, and if you look closely, you will see that although they are bold, they are very simply detailed.

This project is a great one to use your imagination with, as the simple but effective techniques give you a basis for decorative application. Yet at the same time they call out for you to experiment with different colours, patterns and even characters.

Preparation and tips

● Prepare the chest for painting according to the instructions on page 15. Be sure to sand the edges, both top and bottom, very carefully as the box will be used by children. You may also wish to run the sandpaper along all of the outside edges to round them slightly, making them even safer and less likely to splinter.

● When the wood is cleaned and prepared, apply two coats of white undercoat, allowing the first to dry before applying the second. After each coat has dried, sand the entire piece lightly with fine-grade sandpaper or wire wool to create a smooth finish, taking care not to remove patches of paint.

Materials and equipment

Wooden toy box

1 litre (32 fl oz) undercoat: white

1 litre (32 fl oz) vinyl matt emulsion: light blue

60 ml (2 fl oz) acrylic paints: purple, dark blue, creamy yellow, white, orange

Paintbrushes: 2.5 cm (1 in) household; variety of detail

Sponge

Coping saw

Pencil

Brass panel pins (approximately 4 per cat) and/or white glue

Hammer

1 litre (32 fl oz) poly-gloss varnish

Fine-grade sandpaper/wire wool

▲ **1** Paint the front panel of the box with a thin layer of light blue vinyl matt emulsion. Before it has dried, lightly dab the painted area with a sponge, progressing evenly from one side of the panel to the other, creating a textural effect.

On the base of the box, use the same light blue that was used for the panel. Instead of sponging, follow with a purple acrylic and, using the end of the brush, stipple lightly over the blue.

▲ **2** Paint in the top and the front borders. Dark blue is used here.

Border the top and front panel in a bright colour. This will offset the top, and frame the front. A creamy yellow is used here.

◀ **3** Making sure that the dark areas at the top and front are dry, randomly paint stars of varying sizes over the box, or any other detail you may wish to use. The stars here are painted by using two overlapping triangles in white acrylic. You may wish to make light pencil marks where you want your details to go before you begin painting.

Using the orange striping shown to the left, or a detail of your choice, accent the lightly painted moulding around the top.

▲ **4** The cats, or any animal of your choice (see the ducks shown on the floral bed on page 86, for example) are traced onto pieces of 4 mm (¹/₆ in) birchfaced plywood and cut out with a coping saw. You may find it helpful to make a template out of thin paper cardboard and then trace the animals onto the plywood. (See the paper cardboard template technique that is described on page 13.)

Be sure to sand both the front and the edges carefully, and then give each animal one coat of white acrylic, being sure to paint the edges as well. When the white has dried, you can decorate your animal any way you may wish.

▲ **5** Alternatively, if you don't wish to use wooden cut-outs, paint the animals directly onto the box. Use a cardboard or wood template, trace the animals onto the box and paint them with white acrylic, allowing it to dry thoroughly before you begin the fun part of the decorating.

◄ **6** When the cut-outs are decorated and have dried thoroughly, attach them to the box with brass panel pins. Be sure that they are secure, as children will inevitably try to get their fingers behind them and pull them off. You may wish to use white glue as well as the panel pins for extra strength. As a final detail, you might personalize the toy box with the child's name, or a label such as 'DAVID'S TOYS'.

When you are completely finished and all the paint has dried thoroughly, give the entire box one coat of a standard poly-gloss varnish to seal and protect the paint. Try to cover evenly, being careful not to let the varnish accumulate around the edges of the wooden animals, or to leave drip marks in the finish.

Dutch Folk Cradle

By Dave and Kaye Ball

A beautiful rocking cradle or crib like this is sure to become a family heirloom. The Dutch folk motif and colours used are simple and classic, but you may wish to adapt a colour scheme or choose a design that is more fitting to the decor of your baby's room. When your baby has outgrown the cradle, use it as a store for toys or soft animals.

Preparation and tips

● Prepare the cradle for painting according to the instructions on page 15. Be sure to sand the entire piece very carefully as it will be used by children. You may also wish to run the sandpaper along all of the outside edges to round them slightly, making them a bit safer and less likely to splinter.

● When the wood is cleaned and prepared, apply one coat of white to the inside (buttermilk was used here), and one coat of a brick red (tawny) to the outside. Be aware that some paints contain lead and are therefore toxic if ingested. Check with your paint dealer when buying paints for furniture that will be used by children. A safe bet is generally to choose water-based acrylics. When the paints have dried, sand over lightly with sandpaper, being careful not to remove patches of paint.

Materials and equipment

Cradle

1 litre (32 fl oz) undercoat: white

1 litre (32 fl oz) vinyl matt emulsions: tawny red, holly green, buttermilk

37 ml (1 1/4 fl oz) oil paints:light blue, grass green, light green, grey, white, raw umber, yellow ochre

Paintbrushes: 2.5 cm (1 in) household; stencil; Nos 4, 6 and 8 artist's detail

Carbon paper

Masking tape

Ballpoint pen

Medium-grade wire wool

Mellow wax

Sandpaper

▶ **2** Wearing a protective glove, use a medium grade of wire wool and rub over the entire piece, concentrating particularly on the areas where the wax was applied. This will expose patches of the red undercoat. Wipe off paint and wood dust before beginning the next step.

▲ **1** To create the distressed areas, rub beeswax into those places where there would most likely be wearing over time, such as around the handles and at the edges.

Leave the wax to dry, then give the outside of the cradle one coat of holly green emulsion. Allow to dry thoroughly.

▼ **3** Take the drawn or photocopied design you have chosen and position it onto the cradle with a piece of carbon paper underneath, and secure both in place with masking tape. Trace over your design with a ballpoint pen, taking care not to press too hard as you may leave an impression in the wood. Before you remove the design, pull one corner away and check to see that the drawing has transferred completely. If it has not, carefully replace the corner, and you should be able to retrace without creating double lines.

▲ **4** Begin by filling in your design with solid blocks of colour. No. 6 and No. 8 detail brushes work well for this. Allow it to dry thoroughly before you begin detailing. For detailed work, a No. 4 detail brush works well.

▶ **5** To finish, use two coats of mellow wax which will seal the paint and give the decoration a soft lustre.

Chicken Cushion

By Freddie Roberts

Animal motifs such as dogs, cats and birds have long adorned soft furnishings. This tradition may be very successfully adapted by using such imagery to make shaped cushions where the design is applied to heavy cotton with paper stencils. Traditionally, pigment is dabbed onto cloth with a natural sponge or a stencilling brush through a thin cardboard or steel stencil. Here, the stencilling process is speeded up by using a small silk screen and rubber squeegee. If the thin paper stencil is handled carefully, it may be used several times over to make sets of cushions.

Preparation and tips

● To make the first stencil, draw the body of the chicken (minus the feet, beak, comb and wattle) in the centre of a large sheet of paper. Place the paper on a firm surface or cutting mat and carefully cut out the body area using a craft knife. Discard the inner silhouette and keep the cut-out sheet. Place the second sheet of paper under the first and trace around the inside edge of the cut-out body area. Remove the first stencil. Add a beak, comb, wattle and feet to the second chicken shape.
● Place the sheet of paper on a hard surface or cutting mat and carefully cut out the whole chicken shape using a craft knife. This cut-out silhouette is the second stencil. The surrounding paper may be discarded.

Materials and equipment

1 m (40 in) washed and bleached cotton

Pencil

2 large sheets of paper, same size as or slightly larger than the silk-screen

Craft knife

Masking tape

50 x 65 cm (20 x 26 in) fabric-printing silk screen

Screen-printing fabric ink: green, brown

Squeegee: to fit screen width

Plastic spatula

Fabric pens: various colours

Puffy fabric pen: black

Iron

Washable stuffing (batting)

Pins, needle and thread

Rubber gloves

▼ **1** Prepare the print surface as directed. Pin or tape the cotton in position, ensuring that the fabric is taut and smooth. Place the first stencil on the fabric close to the selvage and fix it in position with masking tape. Place the prepared screen on top of the stencil.

▲ **2** Wearing rubber gloves to protect your hands from ink stains, pour 100 ml (4 fl oz) of brown ink evenly down one edge of the screen into the area that forms the reservoir. Place the squeegee onto the screen behind the line of ink. Hold it at an angle of 45 degrees and pull the ink towards you across the screen using a swift, firm motion, pressing down slightly as you pull.

When you reach the other side of the screen pour a little more ink in if necessary, this time in the opposite reservoir. Place the squeegee behind the ink as before, and, again at an angle of 45 degrees, repeat the printing process, this time pushing the squeegee away from you. When you reach the other side of the screen, rest the squeegee against it and carefully lift it off the fabric, removing one side of the screen first, and then the other.

Scrape any excess ink off the screen and squeegee using a plastic spatula. Peel the stencil from the screen. Wash the squeegee and screen immediately after printing and leave them to dry.

▲ **3** To print the green border around the chicken, wait until the screen has dried, then place the second stencil on top of the printed brown chicken body shape so that it is completely masked. As before, place the screen on top of the stencil. Pour 150 ml (5 fl oz) green ink evenly along one edge of the screen and, again, print twice, adding more ink as necessary. After you have lifted the screen off the fabric, carefully peel the stencil away from the screen.

Place the screen onto the other half of the cotton, pour a line of green ink along one side of the screen, and print a plain rectangle of green fabric. This will eventually be used to make the back of the cushion. Remove the screen and clean thoroughly.

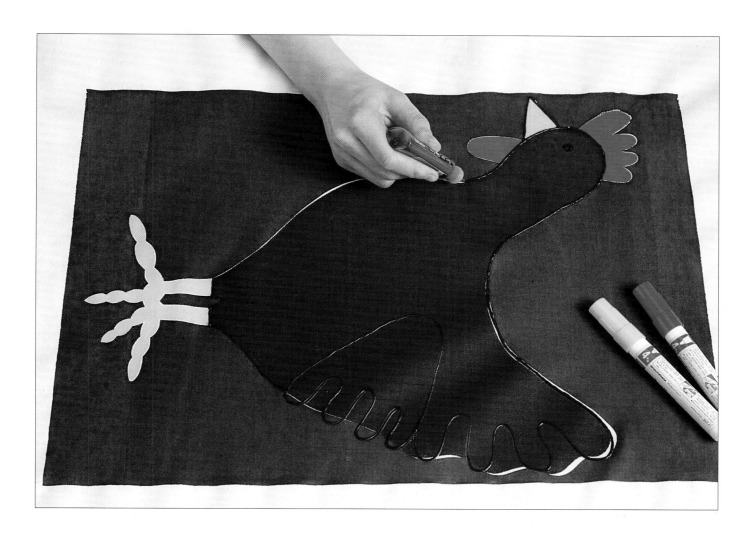

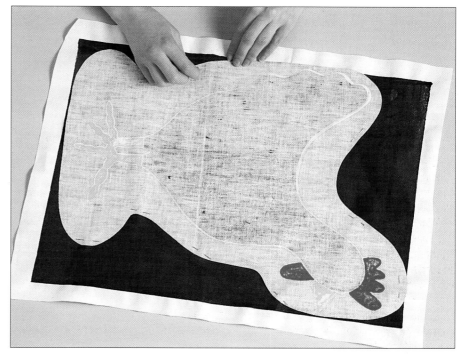

▲ **4** Allow the chicken to dry thoroughly and then, using fabric pens, colour the beak, comb and wattle. When the ink has dried, outline the body and wings and draw in the chicken's eye with a black puffy fabric pen. Cover the painted and printed areas with a clean pressing cloth and steam the fabric to fix according to the manufacturer's instructions.

▶ **5** Cut around the printed chicken and green border leaving a 4 cm (1¹/₂ in) seam allowance. Place the chicken on the green rectangular back and cut around it. Pin the two pieces together, with right sides facing, and firmly sew, leaving an 8 cm (3¹/₂ in) opening at the chicken's feet.

Clip the curved seam line and then turn the cushion the right way out. Stuff firmly, and slip stitch the opening.

Graphic Cotton Curtains

By Melanie Williams

Stencilling strong colours and motifs onto very plain, inexpensive fabric is a great way to transform it into a striking tablecloth or curtain. This natural cotton fabric has been worked with a bold, graphic border made up from layers of simple shapes. The curtain is hung from easy-to-make loops. Although a template is given here, there is no reason why you should not draw inspiration from elsewhere and create your own motifs and images.

Preparation and tips

● Trace the patterns below and transfer them to the stencil paper. Cut out the stencils using a scalpel (x-acto knife) as described on page 15.

Use a photocopier to enlarge these patterns by 166%

Materials and equipment

Lightweight cotton fabric to fit window area

Stencil paper

Fabric paints: various colours

Natural sponge

Coloured thread

Masking tape

Iron

Sewing machine (optional)

Pins

Tracing paper

Pencil

Scalpel (x-acto knife)

Palette or saucers

▶ **1** Mix up some yellow paint in a saucer. Secure the border stencil close to the edge of the fabric using strips of masking tape. Sponge the stencil with yellow and repeat around the edge of the fabric. Press with a warm iron when the paint is almost dry.

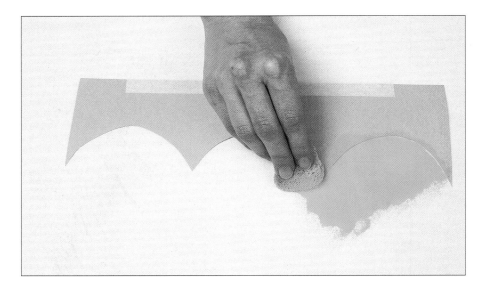

▶ **2** In another saucer, mix up a little red paint. Tape the heart stencil into one of the scallops on the border and secure with tape. Sponge the heart with red, carefully lifting off the stencil and repeating the motif in every alternate scallop. Press with a warm iron when the paint is almost dry.

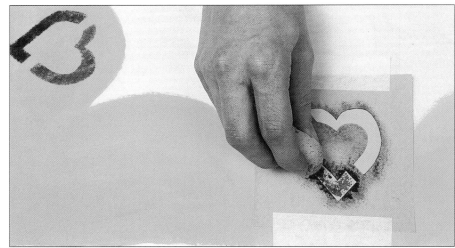

◀ **3** Mix up some blue paint and tape the dot stencil into one of the spaces between the hearts. Sponge the dot with blue, lift off and repeat around the border, filling in all the gaps to complete the design. Press with a warm iron once more.

Use the same dot stencil to sponge red, yellow and blue paint over the curtain, wiping the stencil clean between applications. When you are pleased with the design, press the fabric with a warm iron.

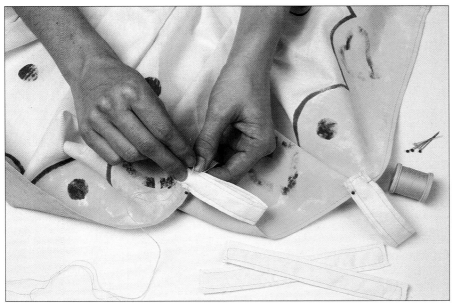

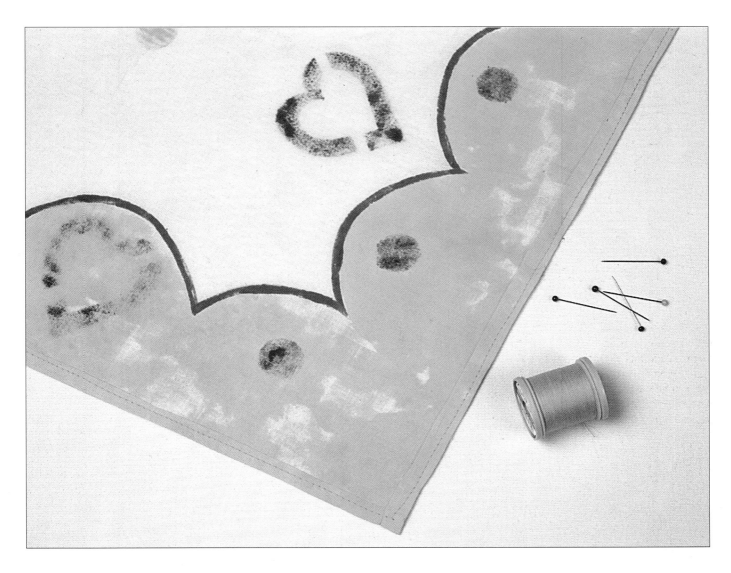

▲ **4** Press a small double hem all around the curtain, pinning the hem in place as you go. Either stitch the hem by hand or, for speed, use a sewing machine.

◀ **5** To make the hanging loops, cut the remaining fabric into 17 x 9 cm (6 ¹/₂ x 3 ¹/₂ in) strips. (You will not need many; for this small curtain, five loops were sufficient.) Fold each strip lengthwise, bringing both long sides into the centre. Press and fold in half lengthwise once more. Stitch along the side to secure it. Repeat this procedure for each loop.

Using a tape measure to help you, position the loops at equal distances along the top of the curtain, tuck under the raw edges and hand sew in place.

Papier Mâché Mobile

By Julie Arkell

This colourful mobile, with its rainbow of thin ribbons, is not only delightful to look at, but when hung in a place that catches a slight draught, will produce a soft, soothing, clicking sound.

Here a variety of motifs have been chosen: dog, sun, fish, clown and a heart, but you could choose just one design – a fish, for instance – and decorate the pieces differently to give variety of colour.

The pieces are light enough to hang from a wooden framework that is simply stuck together with glue. When inserting the screw eyes into the cardboard templates, make sure that you find the balancing point of each piece, unless you intend them to hang at angles.

Preparation and tips

- Use quick-drying epoxy resin to glue the wooden hanger together, and to glue the screw eyes to the mobile shapes.
- Apply the paste with your hand to one side of the paper. Apply two layers of paper pieces to the framework and the mobile shapes, allowing about 24 hours' drying time between the layers. Dry on a wire rack to allow air to pass around the pieces.
- Assemble the materials. Have the wood cut to the required lengths, or cut it yourself with a hacksaw. Cut out the cardboard shapes with scissors. The pieces are all about 10-13 cm (4-5 in) long.
- Tear the newspaper into pieces about 5-8 cm (2-3 in) long.

Materials and equipment

38 cm (15 in) square corrugated cardboard

Felt-tip pen or pencil

Scissors

11 screw eyes

Quick-drying epoxy resin

Two 15 cm x 12 mm (6 x ½ in) softwood

Small hacksaw to cut wood (if necessary)

Newspaper

Bowl

Wallpaper paste (mixed)

Wire rack

Emulsion paint: white

Gouache paints: various colours

Polyurethane varnish

Paintbrushes: household, artist's

Five 30 cm (12 in) long thin ribbons: various colours

▶ **1** Glue the two pieces of wood together to form a cross. Push the shank of five screw eyes into the corrugations of the mobile shapes and glue in place. Screw five screw eyes into the ends and middle of one side of the wooden framework and one eye into the middle on the other side.

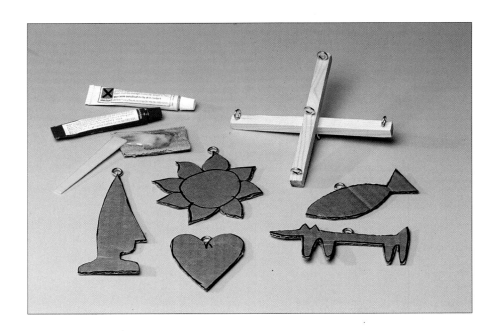

▼ **2** Cover the framework and the shapes with two layers of pasted newspaper pieces, keeping the eyes clear, and dry them on a wire rack.
  Using the household paintbrush, give the framework and the shapes a coat of white emulsion paint and allow to dry.

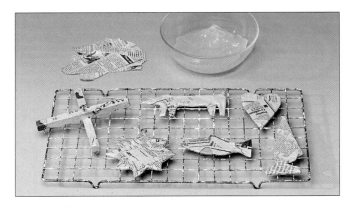

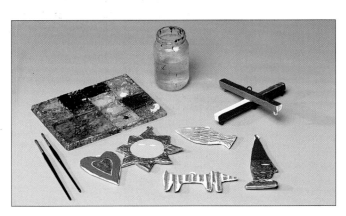

▲ **3** Using the artist's brushes, decorate the pieces with gouache paint, leaving the first coat to dry before applying subsequent layers and decorative details.

▲ **4** When dry, give all the pieces a coat of gloss varnish and allow to dry. Then assemble the mobile, tying the ribbon with double knots. Cut the ribbons to the required lengths, making the central piece hang higher than the rest.
  All that remains is to hang your mobile in a place where it catches a slight draught.

Suppliers

United Kingdom

L Cornelissen & Son Ltd
105 Great Russell Street
London
WC1B 3RY
Tel: 020 7636 1045
(manufacturers and retailers of
materials for painters, pastellists,
gilders and printmakers)

J W Bollom & Co Ltd
Croydon Road
Beckenham
Kent
BR3 4BL
Tel: 020 8658 2299
(paints)

Cole & Son Ltd
Lifford House
199 Eade Road
London
N4 1DN
Tel: 020 8442 8844
(paints)

Dylon International Ltd
Worsley Bridge Road
Lower Sydenham
London
SE26 5HD
Tel: 020 8663 4801
(fabric paints and specialist pens)

T N Lawrence & Son Ltd
208 Portland Road
Hove
East Sussex
BN3 5QT
Tel: 01273 260 260
(printmaking tools, papers and
specialist papers)

**Lyn Le Grice Stencil
Design Ltd**
The Flower Loft
Trereife
Penzance
Cornwall
TR20 8TJ
Tel: 01736 364 193
(pre-cut stencils)

Omnihome Ltd
32 Chamberlayne Road
London NW10 3JE
Tel: 020 8968 2048
(oil colours, brushes and varnishes)

Potterycrafts Ltd
Campbell Road
Stoke-On-Trent
Staffordshire
ST4 4ET
Tel: 01782 745 000
(supplier of white china 'blanks'
and ceramic kilns)

Stuart R Stevenson
68 Clerkenwell Road
London EC1M 5QA
Tel: 020 7253 1693
(gold and silver leaf, brushes and
complete selection of gilding materials)

Titian Studio
32 Warple Way
London
W3 0DJ
Tel: 020 8222 6600
(gilders)

Wiggins Teape
Gateway House
Philippa Way
Leeds
West Yorkshire
LS12 6LS
Tel: 0113 259 8299
(wide range of machine-made paper
and cardboard)

New Zealand

Auckland Decorative Arts
591 Remuera Road
Upland Village
Auckland
Tel: 09 524 0936

Resene Colour Shops
Branches throughout New Zealand.
Check your local Yellow or White Pages
Tel: 09 444 4387
www.resene.co.nz

Studio Art Supplies
81 Parnell Rise
Parnell
Auckland
Tel: 09 377 0302

NZ Hobby Clay & Craft Co
1/180 James Fletcher Drive
Mangere
Tel: 09 270 0140

Australia

Lincraft
For branches contact:
Head Office
31-33 Alfred St
Blackburn
VIC 3130

Premier Art Supplies
43 Gilles Street
Adelaide
South Australia 5000
Tel: 08 8212 5922

United States

For general paint stockists in the
United States, contact your local
major paint suppliers, such as
Sinclair Paints, Sherwin William
Paints, Pearl,Majestic Painter Center
or your nearest art and craft stores

Rupert Gibbon & Spider Inc
1147 Healdsburg Avenue
Healdsburg
CA 95448-3405
Tel: 707 433 9577

Daniel Smith Inc
4150 First Avenue South
Seattle
WA 98134-2302
Tel: 206 223 9599